WHAT PRICE ZION

Carol Partridge McIntosh
Carole Osborne Cole

Deseret Book Company
Salt Lake City, Utah

© 1983 Deseret Book Company
All rights reserved
Printed in the United States of America
First printing January 1983

Library of Congress Cataloging in Publication Data
McIntosh, Carol Partridge.
   What price Zion.
   1. Mormons—History—Fiction.   I. Cole,
Carole Osborne.   II. Title.
PS3563.C3695W48   1983   813'.54   82-23567
ISBN 0-87747-927-5

To the memory of Lydia Littlefield McNiven, for without her this story could not have been told

1

Autumn 1842

Yet we'll share joy and sorrow with thee
Hymns, no. 145

"Ann, it's me! Are you home?" The door opened tentatively and Sarah Toomer stuck her head through the narrow crack. She'd come round to the kitchen door. From her limited vantage point she could see all there was of the windowless room—a cooking area over which hung a single pot used to cook everything from the morning's gruel to a holiday boiled mutton and cabbage; open shelves that lined the walls and were stacked neatly with a mismatched assortment of crockery, utensils, and tins of sugar, tea, and a few spices and condiments; and a rough-board table that stood precariously on three legs, its fourth leg too short to help the others. Four chairs in similar uneven circumstances surrounded the table.

"Come in, come," Ann called from the bedroom. "I'm feeding Fanny."

Sarah bustled into the room as two small children tumbled into the kitchen from the parlor. The salty scent of the sea air rushed full into the room.

"How're my darlin's today?" Sarah embraced them heartily.

They teetered expectantly in front of her. Sarah stood quietly, amused at their anticipation. "And what're you standing there for?" she said in mock sternness.

Their eyes fell, and they looked at one another.

"We thought . . ." Johnny began.

"Please, auntie . . ." young Sarah Jane stammered.

The disappointment in their eyes melted their aunt's heart, and she gathered them once again in a fierce embrace. "Here now, here's your treat. You didn't really think I'd not bring you one?"

She folded the sweet into their waiting hands, and with their ha'penny treacle clutched tightly, Johnny and Sarah Jane returned happily to their play. Sarah popped her head around the bedroom door and called to Ann.

"How's our sweet babe today?" Sarah cooed as she watched Ann nursing the infant. Unaware of the picture they made, Ann sat on the edge of the bed holding Fanny to her breast. The bed took up the larger part of the room. A single high window covered with rather limp lace curtains allowed only a limited amount of light from the northern exposure.

Sarah moved closer and traced the curve of the baby's soft cheek with a gentle finger. "She's a beauty, Ann," Sarah sighed. "John will be a proud one."

"I can't wait for him to see her," Ann replied. She brushed a silky wisp of coal-black hair from the baby's brow. "This trip seems so much longer for some reason. I'm sure it's because I want so much to show Fanny off to him. Five months since he sailed, but he said the *Victor*'d probably not be in port again until late October."

"Ah, the sailor's life!" Sarah smiled.

"It's the sailor's wife's life that's to be lamented," Ann retorted.

"It won't be long now, Ann, and you'll be holding your sailor man in your arms, and he'll be filling your head with his stories."

The two sisters chatted quietly for a while, exchanging family gossip; then when Fanny had filled herself so full that a tiny trickle of milk overflowed a corner of her mouth, she relaxed her hold on her mother's breast and promptly fell asleep. Ann laid Fanny on the bed and put herself to rights.

"Sarah, be a dear and take Johnny and your namesake to market for me. I'll be needing a few things for supper, and I don't want to take Fanny out just now."

Sarah agreed good-naturedly and gathered up the two oldest Fry children. Ann handed Sarah a list and a few shillings, gave the children a kiss and admonitions, and saw them all off at the door.

"You stay for a bite when you come back, Sarah," Ann called to their retreating figures.

All three turned to wave and nod, and Ann closed the door against the autumn air, crisp with a sea breeze from the channel. The breeze had cleared away the earlier foggy air.

The small house near the sea that John Fry loved so much was generally warm and comfortable and boasted a larger-than-usual parlor window through which the sunshine poured. The window helped a great deal to keep the house warm—when the sun cooperated. When the sun was hidden by clouds and hampered by gray skies, Ann had to keep the fire in the grate burning steadily.

On this September afternoon the sun had done its job well, and the small parlor was warm and cozy. Ann drew a high-backed chair into the path of the sun's rays and sat for a moment surveying her small domain. Fanny slept peacefully in the tiny, hand-carved cradle John had brought home from one of his voyages. Reaching out a foot, Ann gently set the cradle to rocking. Fanny puckered her tiny mouth, heaved a deep, shuddering sigh, and slept on. A little hand reached out, its five tiny fingers forming a soft star.

It was a small house, with only a parlor, tiny kitchen, and one bedroom. Johnny and young Sarah slept on the battered sofa in the parlor, one at each end, a single blanket stretched to cover both. It would not be long before Fanny would outgrow the tiny cradle, and they would need a place for her to sleep. Somehow they'd have to find a larger place for their burgeoning family. Ann resolved to speak to John about it as soon as he returned. She would not mind moving inland a bit farther. The damp air and coastal fog often made the winters difficult and cold.

Ann smiled as she thought of the previous winter. There had been a spell of several overcast days. The large parlor window had framed only drizzly, cloudy weather for days. John had been at sea, and the voyage was longer than expected. Ann's funds had dipped to a worrisome low, and she had kept herself, Johnny, and Sarah bundled in extra clothes to avoid burning their meager supply of coal too quickly. It was Sarah who had rescued them. She'd appeared at the door with a huge hunk of coal cradled in her arms, her face smudged where she'd brushed back a lock of hair. She'd made a comical, but so very welcome sight.

"One lump, or two, m'um?" she'd mimicked.

Sarah always seemed to be there. Ann was the younger of the two sisters, with two brothers, William and James, also older than Ann, William by just a year. But it was Sarah who kept a watchful eye over her younger sister, especially when John was at sea.

They were an odd-looking pair of sisters. Where Sarah was tall, angular, outspoken, and effusive, Ann was shorter, softer, and rounder, in appearance as well as manner. Ann spoke quietly and carefully, keeping in check a temper that could flare fiercely when provoked. Sarah seemed to have no temper—always evenly balanced, speaking her mind freely and sharing whatever emotion she felt at the moment with little or no inhibition.

For the hundredth time Ann wondered why a decent man hadn't come along and snatched up Sarah for a wife. If the right man could only see her with Johnny and Sarah, Ann thought to herself. "It's a proper mother she'll make," she said aloud. "She needs a man like my John." Her toe continued to rock Fanny's cradle. "Ah, John, my dear, I hope it's soon you'll be getting home."

The sun continued its steady radiance, and Ann closed her eyes, basking in its comfort. Imperceptibly at first, then increasingly, a chill settled over her. She opened her eyes, expecting to see the sun covered by a cloud. But the sun still streamed, unobstructed, through the window. But suddenly Ann felt cold, as though an icy hand had gripped the center of her being and extended its chilly fingers, drawing away her body's warmth.

Instinctively she reached to check Fanny. She stroked the velvet cheek and felt the warm little body. The baby squirmed slightly, and her rosebud mouth curved into a tiny smile.

Fanny was fine. Ann shook herself. *Whatever is the matter with me,* she thought impatiently. *One moment I feel warm and content, the next as though, as though . . .*

Ann tucked the blanket carefully around the sleeping infant. She pushed her thoughts away from the gloom that had unaccountably overtaken her, and forced herself into the kitchen to start the cooking fire and begin preparations for supper.

Sarah, Johnny, and little Sarah returned with their usual energy, full of market news and gossip. Ann listened as she worked while Sarah chattered along with the children.

"Old Crawford is getting gruffer by the day," Sarah confided.

"He was that cross with me, Mum," Johnny confirmed.

"Cross," little Sarah echoed, and popped a thumb into her mouth. Her other hand twirled a strand of brown hair.

Ann only smiled and nodded.

During the evening meal Sarah spoke her mind. "Ann, are you ill? You seem so quiet."

"La, and I'm fine. I'm missing John is all." She shrugged.

Sarah studied her sister for a moment. Her round face seemed pinched, and the blue-gray eyes held a bewilderment, almost a fear. Ann seemed sincere enough in her protestations of good health, yet Sarah was sure something was bothering her. Sarah made up her mind to watch Ann carefully.

In spite of Ann's uneasy foreboding, the days passed smoothly in their usual routine. Ann marketed, sewed, cleaned house, and nursed her infant. Gradually the gloom evaporated. Sarah stopped by frequently, the news courier for the Toomer family.

"James and his wife are expecting again," she announced one day.

"William is courting another girl," she confided on yet another visit.

"That William. He's as particular as you, Sarah. I don't know if he'll ever marry," Ann chided.

And on one visit in November, Sarah burst through the door without even her customary tentative door opening.

"Ann, Ann, the *Victor* is in the harbor!"

"Oh, Sarah, are you sure it's John's ship—the *Victor?*"

"Yes, yes, you must hurry. He'll be here soon!"

"Have I time to run to market?" Ann seemed suddenly flustered.

"Go, I'll stay here with the children."

Ann's face flushed with excitement and the prospect of seeing John once again. Her mind's eye pictured his tall lanky frame in the doorway, that cocky grin splitting his face from ear to ear, his bag thrown over his shoulder.

"Ann, don't stand there dreaming, girl, get on with your marketing," Sarah chided her.

Ann blushed and hugged Sarah. "I'll be back before you know it." She gathered up her wrap and marketing bag and fairly flew down the twisted street. By the time she returned Sarah had tidied up and dusted the house, and had even washed the children's faces and hands and combed their hair. Even Fanny's dark locks sported a tiny red bow, held precariously in place with a drop of molasses. The table was set, too, the cooking fire crackled, and a bowl of biscuit dough had been started.

"Here now, you take over. I'm going to pop off before I get caught in the midst of your homecoming." Sarah pulled the apron from her waist and tied on her bonnet. She threw her cape over her shoulders, embraced Ann, called goodbye to the children, and moved quickly to the door.

"Sarah, you're a dear. I don't know what I'd do without you."

Sarah smiled, threw a kiss, and was gone.

The smell of fresh vegetables and boiled mutton shank drew the children into the kitchen. Ann held them off as long as she could, but finally sat them up to the table and fed them. In snatched moments between the bustle of getting ready, she ran to the bedroom and changed into a fresh dress, one she knew John admired, and redid her hair. It seemed to be taking an unusually long time to dock the ship and release the crew. But surely John would burst through the door at any moment.

Ann waited. The clock ticked steadily in the parlor. The children tired of the wait and fussed, and at last Ann put them to bed. The ticking clock grew louder and louder. Where was he? It wasn't like him to stop at a pub—he'd always come straight home. She tucked the blanket snugly around the children for the tenth time, then took a chair by the window, staring for a time at the circle of light pooled around the gas streetlamp. She couldn't bear to sit for long, though, and so she left the chair and paced anxiously.

She was tempted to run through the twisted, cobbled streets to the docks. She wanted to wait at the foot of the gangplank and watch John stride long-leggedly down to gather her into his arms and crush her to him in a mighty homecoming embrace. But she could not leave the sleeping children. *What could be keeping him?*

The knock on the door startled her. She hurried to open it. A young sailor filled the open doorway, his beefy hands twisting his cap.

"Beggin' your pardon, m'um. Would this be Private John Fry's 'ome?"

"Yes," Ann nodded. "I'm Ann Fry. John Fry's my husband."

"I'm sorry, m'um, I 'ates to tell you this, but the cap'n, 'e sent me wi' this." He held out an envelope.

Ann stared at it briefly, then took it and tore it open. The message was carefully written in a large scrawl.

"It is with deep regret that I must inform you of the loss of Private John Fry in a storm at sea on September 30, 1842 . . . "

The rest of the message became a blur. Ann rocked briefly on her feet, and the young sailor grabbed her by both elbows and steered her toward a chair near the kitchen table.

"Can I get someone for you, m'um? A neighbor?"

"No, no, I'm fine. I'll be fine." Her ashen face put the lie to her words.

The young sailor stared at her. "I'll fetch anyone you want, Mrs. Fry, just say where and 'oo."

"Please, I'll be all right. You needn't stay." Ann extended a trembling hand and touched the sailor gently on his arm.

"You're sure now, I do 'ave some other messages . . ." He backed carefully out of the room.

Ann watched the door shut slowly. She stared again at the envelope in her hand, seeming to see its awful message right through the paper. The chilly hand that had overwhelmed her a few weeks before returned once again to snatch her body's warmth. Its familiar gloom settled all around her, and Ann recognized now its intended message.

"Lost at sea, lost at sea," the phrase echoed through her being.

"But he's never seen the baby," she protested aloud.

That doesn't matter, the answer came back. *He's lost at sea, lost at sea.*

And comprehending at last, Ann dropped her head to the table and wept.

2

Early 1843 to October 1846

Hushed be the accents of sorrow and mourning
Hymns, no. 182

"I'm not sure, Sarah," Ann mused. "I'm not sure what to do."

"It will be good for you, Ann. It'll bring in a little money above John's pension and keep you too busy to think," Sarah argued.

"However did you think of a laundry business?"

"La, and I've done a bit of work on that, Ann," Sarah declared. "I've enquired about and there's no one I can find behither the finer homes in this part of town where anybody else is doing laundry. Why can't we?"

Sarah had been pressuring Ann for several days to make this decision. Ann could tell that Sarah was worried about her. Ann had been so distant with her—and the children. She seemed to shrink from them, especially from Johnny.

When there was no reply from Ann, Sarah went on. "I'm beazled with cleaning other people's houses, Ann. I want a change."

"Are you sure cleaning other people's clothes is the answer?"

"It's not the nature of the work, but the idea we'll be working for us, not for someone else. We'll be our own bosses," Sarah urged.

Ann sighed. She could see Sarah was not going to relent on this. "Sarah, give me just a little more time. It's not been that long since— since—"

8

"Since John's death," Sarah finished for her. "But the sooner you take up the pieces, the sooner life will put itself to rights again."

Dear Sarah, Ann thought. *She wants so desperately to help me.* Aloud, Ann vacillated some more. "Give me a few more days, dear. I promise I'll let you know definitely by nexdy at the latest."

Sarah sighed and made ready to leave. "Take care, then. I'll see you soon."

"Sarah, I appreciate what you're trying to do." Ann looked into Sarah's brown eyes.

The two sisters communicated wordlessly for a moment before hugging one another, then said goodbye.

Ann turned back to her thoughts. It had been only a matter of weeks since news of John's death. Somehow she had muddled through the memorial service, and Christmas. Now the enormity of her loss was beginning to make itself felt in the everyday hum of Ann's existence. There was a strong tendency to want to ignore the evidence of John's death, to pretend that he was still at sea, that he would be home soon, embracing the children, exclaiming over little Fanny, regaling Ann with stories, kissing her tenderly, and loving her with his usual urgency. It would have been fairly easy to forget the young sailor's visit and the carefully worded message from the captain, to just pretend the visit had never happened, the message never been delivered. After all, Ann was used to days and nights alone, days filled with waiting, living with part of her performing the daily tasks, but part of her living for the day when John came through the door and she felt whole again.

But John would never be home again. As attractive as blotting out the fact of his death appeared to be, Ann knew she could not deceive herself that way. She would accept—had to accept—*needed* to accept her husband's death and begin again with whatever was left of her life.

There *were* the children. Well-wishers' declarations to the contrary, the children had *not* been a comfort to her—they were so much a part of John. She had never considered them as being made of substance from *both* her and John. She had merely been the harbor for their existence, an existence sprung entirely from John and the love they bore one another.

Little Johnny was especially difficult to have around right now. He was a tiny duplicate of his father. He'd even begun to walk like him, and there were times when he cocked his head a certain way when he looked at Ann that tore at Ann's heart—John had looked at her just that way so often.

It was a source of amazement to Ann that little Johnny could not only look but act so much like his father, especially since John had been gone from home so much of Johnny's life. Ann studied her son as he played with a small carved replica of the *Victor* that a shipmate of John's had brought to the house. A shock of sandy hair haloed Johnny's face, and an unruly lock fell over one eye. It pained Ann with jarring memories to look at him, yet she loved him, too—he was all she had left of John. As if he sensed his mother's thoughts, Johnny raised his eyes to hers.

"I'm sorry, Mum," he said.

"Why, whatever for, son?" she answered, surprised.

"I'm sorry our daddy won't be home no more," Johnny murmured. "I'm sorry it's made you so sad. Did it happen because I was angry with Sarah?"

Ann knelt down and gathered her small son to her and rested her head on his. "Hush, you mustn't think that. Daddy's not coming home not because of anything we did or didn't do. 'Tis God's will, that's all. And we mustn't question it." Ann held her boy tightly. "How would you like to be my special helper," Ann fought back tears as she spoke. "We've got a big job to do together, and you can be my man around the house."

Johnny nodded his head. "I'll be yer man, Mum," he declared soberly.

Ann laughed a bit through an emotion-constricted throat. "And quite a man at that." She hugged him again.

His body was warm and momentarily comforting, but then, as had happened so often before, unbidden, came the awful mental pictures of John's foundering in the sea, fighting for his life against the crashing waves, sinking and groping his way to the surface again and again before finally exhausting his strength and letting the sea take him to its green, fathomless depths. Ann squeezed her eyes tightly shut, forcing the awful pictures away from her. Gradually the haunting scenes faded, and she pushed Johnny away to hold him at arm's length. She shook him slightly as she vowed fiercely, "But you'll never be lost at sea, Johnny. No son of mine will ever go to sea! I'll wager my own life on that!"

The laundry business gradually prospered. Sarah and little Johnny had canvassed the bigger, fancier homes in a wide radius from the Fry house, leaving with the kitchen help small printed handbills declaring the availability of their services. Johnny was excited to be of help and made an impressive little messenger wearing his own neatly laundered and pressed clothes.

The sisters worked well together. Sarah never complained when Ann had to take time to care for the children or to quiet a small spat. She was good company, and in her effusive, enthusiastic way drew Ann gradually back to living with at least a surface effort at happiness. In the early months their conversation had been spotty, and usually centered around Ann's memories of John. Sarah sensed Ann's need to reinforce her memories, and nodded, encouraged, sympathized, and laughed in all the right places. Only when Ann realized she was repeating the same stories did she conclude it was time to put John's memory away in the privacy of her heart and draw it out only when she was alone. She had talked away much of the hurt. It was time to take up living in the present.

"Sarah, I'll deliver this basket to the Parker house before I go on to market," Ann declared one day.

"Good enough, Ann. We didn't promise them before tomorrow, so they'll be glad we're ahead of schedule," Sarah responded from behind her sadirons. "And bring back a bit of fruit; I've a hankering for a plum tart."

"That sweet tooth will begin to tell on you one of these days," Ann cautioned. Actually it was Ann who tended more toward loss of her waistline.

The Parker servants were indeed pleased to receive the laundry ahead of the promised time, and the housekeeper added an extra coin to the agreed rate. Then she said, "There's another 'ouse a bit from 'ere who've 'eard of ye, and want ye to call on 'em." She walked out to the street and pointed out the house to Ann. "It's the big 'ouse with the fancy iron gate on the left 'and side of the way. Just through the gate and ask for Mrs. Morfin—she's expectin' ye to call."

Ann thanked the housekeeper for the reference and carried her now-empty basket to the house indicated. Mrs. Morfin had indeed been waiting and refilled the basket with a hefty amount of laundry. A brief haggle over the price brought satisfaction to both Ann and Mrs. Morfin, and Ann departed with her load for market.

The market bustled and milled with shoppers. Ann liked the liveliness of it and the usually good-natured (except for old Crawford) give-and-take between customer and merchant. The market air was a mishmash of sea smells, fish, spices, teas, and overripe fruits, not really unpleasant for all its heady mixture. At each stop for her marketing needs, Ann put down the basket, made her selection, paid for her wares, then made room for them among the clothes in the basket, which grew heavier and heavier. By the time she reached the end of the market square, Ann could no longer heft the basket under her arm, but could only drag it along in jerks and spurts.

In one such pull to further her progress toward home Ann careened into another shopper.

"I beg your pardon—" Ann began.

"Ann! How are you!" It was Margaret Wixom, a friend from before Ann's marriage to John Fry.

"Margaret! What a delight to see you." Ann was genuinely pleased. Margaret looked as though she had done rather well for herself. Her dress was fashionable for the day, and her bonnet was trimmed in plush velvet. A reticule hung straight from her wrist, indicative of a weighty number of coins concealed within. She looked Ann over carefully.

"I was so sorry to hear of John." Margaret's face clouded briefly before she rushed on. "May I introduce my cousin, Will Littlefield?"

Ann turned to the man Margaret had indicated. He was short, not much taller than Ann herself, of a hefty build. He had a dignified air about him and seemed neat and contained in appearance, and was obviously looking for something he had not yet found in a nearby bookseller's stall. He lifted his head at Margaret's mention of his name.

"Will, this is Ann Fry, a dear friend."

Will nodded almost imperceptibly and said nothing. He returned to his search among the books and periodicals.

Ann nodded also and turned back to Margaret.

"How are you getting along, dear? What is this you are lugging about?"

Ann laughed. "I'm afraid my eyes have been larger than my stomach today. I did not mean to buy so much—and of course, I didn't expect to pick up another order while I was out," Ann tried to explain.

"Order? Do you shop for others?"

"No, no. Sarah and I have our own laundry business. This basket is mostly clothes I'm taking home to launder, and I stopped at market on my way."

"May I carry that for you, Mrs. Fry?" Will Littlefield, done with his look at the stall's offering, spoke at last.

"I wouldn't think of imposing, Mr. Littlefield," Ann objected.

"It's really no imposition," Will insisted.

"Go on, Ann, let him act the gentleman. He's really an old curmudgeon too much of the time," Margaret urged.

Ann blushed unexpectedly, and Will picked up the heavily laden basket.

Margaret excused herself. "I'll just let Will help you with your laundry and be on my own way. Ta-ta!"

She jostled off, unaccountably amused with herself.

Will seemed unperturbed by his abandonment, however, and looked expectantly at Ann.

"Really, Mr. Littlefield, I can manage quite well on my own," Ann demurred.

"I'm sure you can; however, I'd consider it an honor to help," Will pressed.

"Very well, it really isn't far, and if you'll take a cup of tea for your efforts, I'll agree," Ann relented.

"Done." Will nodded and smiled approvingly at Ann. He was agreeably aware of her round, pleasant features, her quick smile, blue-gray eyes, and direct gaze. She met his eyes easily and unabashedly, yet she did not seem bold.

For her part Ann thought Will a pleasant chap, certainly helpful and the gentleman. His hands, she noticed as he lifted the basket, were rough, calloused, and obviously used to hard work, but they were willing hands, and she felt no reluctance to their helping her haul home the unwieldy basket. "It's this way, sir," she pointed and stepped out in the direction indicated.

He seemed disinclined to begin a conversation, so Ann tried. "I hope I didn't interrupt your shopping," she offered.

"No, ma'am, I was merely browsing. Margaret was about to drag me to yet another booth so actually I was rather glad for the interruption. I wanted to see if there was a new Dickens."

"You're a reader, then?" Ann smiled.

"Through and through," Will responded as he shifted his burden to his other side. "Do you enjoy reading?"

"Alas, I'm afraid I read but little, though I'd love to have time to do more."

"This laundry business keeps you occupied, then?" Will seemed genuinely interested.

"Me, and my sister both," Ann replied, suddenly aware of eligible

Sarah at home. "It's been nearly three years now, and we've a nice business built up. My son, Johnny, helps too—when I let him off his studies."

They'd arrived at the Fry home. Ann let herself in the parlor door and hoped Sarah had cleared away the bedclothes from the sofa bed the children still slept on. Now there had been added a small trundle for three-year-old Fanny. Mercifully the blanket had been folded, not entirely neatly, and placed on the end of the trundle.

"Sarah, I've brought home an order from a new client—a Mrs. Morfin across from the Parker place."

Sarah bustled in from the kitchen in time to see Will Littlefield deposit the basket on the parlor floor.

"Mr. Littlefield, may I present my sister Sarah? Sarah, this is Margaret Wixom's cousin, Will."

Sarah nodded and smiled, as did Will.

The three stood awkwardly for a moment, then Ann remembered the tea. "Heavens, Sarah, put on the kettle. I've promised Mr. Littlefield a cuppa for his trouble." Ann whipped off her bonnet and hung her cape on the hook by the door.

Will unwrapped a scarf from around his thick neck and stood idly with it dangling from his hands.

Sarah reached for it. "Let me take that for you, sir—and thank you for helping Ann. She's a little thing to be carting around these baskets. I'm usually the one to be out with the blamey things," Sarah explained.

Sarah drew Will into the kitchen and sat him on the least rickety chair, while Ann put on the kettle and set out the cups. Sarah took down the tea tin.

"What kind of work are you in, Mr. Littlefield," Sarah asked as she and Ann both bustled about.

"I'm an ironmonger, ma'am, in one of the drydocks," Will responded.

The three enjoyed their afternoon tea. Sarah even had a few pennywinkles from the bakery she'd bought to fill her perpetual sweet tooth, and she shared them with Ann and Will.

Ann tried to steer the conversation to Sarah. Sarah could not continue to live her own life in Ann's shadow. Not that Ann was unhappy with the current arrangement, but she felt an obligation— more than an obligation, a sincere desire—to see that Sarah found her own niche, her own family, a man and a life of her own. After gentle probing to be sure Will had no wife hidden away, Ann was sure Will was quite eligible enough.

"Sarah has really been the backbone of this business," Ann extolled her sister. "She's the one who had the idea and made it a success from the beginning."

"Pish and tosh," Sarah remonstrated.

"I'm sure you are both quite capable. But one thing bothers me," Will frowned.

Sarah leaned toward him. "And what might that be?"

"Your work would certainly move along a bit easier if you had a cart to transport those baskets."

"La, and haven't we thought of that?" Sarah slapped the table. "But carts come dear, and it's a while before we'll be putting enough by for such a luxury."

Will stood. "I've taken enough of your time, ladies. Thank you for a most pleasant afternoon," he sought Ann's eyes, "and for rescuing me from Margaret."

"You're welcome to call back, Mr. Littlefield. We found the company pleasant, too," Ann replied, and accompanied him to the door. Sarah, too, invited him to return.

Ann and Sarah spoke of nothing else but his visit for days. It had been a welcome break in their normal routine.

Nearly two weeks later, a knock sounded at the parlor door. Sarah opened it and blushed in surprise. Will Littlefield stood expectantly on the stoop.

3

November 1846 to Autumn 1847

A peaceful habitation, in these the latter days

Hymns, no. 205

"Is Mrs. Fry at home? I've something I'd like to show her," Will explained.

Sarah's face clouded for a moment—it was Ann he really wanted to see. She shrugged off the disappointment. It was not a new experience.

"Ann's in the kitchen, Mr. Littlefield. Come right in," she said pleasantly.

"If it's all the same, Miss Sarah, I'll be taking this around to the kitchen door," and Will indicated an odd contraption behind him.

Sarah nodded, pointed out the alley through which he could access the kitchen, and closed the parlor door.

"Ann," she called as she returned to the kitchen, "open the kitchen door. Mr. Littlefield has come to call on *you.*" The sisters exchanged glances, and Ann knew at once what had transpired. She sighed. She'd not flaunt Will's attention before Sarah, and resolved to move him along quickly.

But her resolve melted away when she saw what Will had brought. He stood aside and pushed the contraption back and forth. It resembled a perambulator—in fact, had once been a perambulator, but most of its black covering had been removed and its frame rebuilt into a low bed with slatted sides. The wheels had been banded with iron to withstand the wear of the cobbled streets. It was an unwieldy looking piece, but Ann and Sarah clapped their hands.

"A laundry cart," they exclaimed in near unison. They examined the invention carefully, pushed and pulled at it, and generally gave unrestrained approval. It was heavy, but would nevertheless make the pickup and delivery of the weighty baskets a much easier task.

"Mr. Littlefield, how can we thank you?" Ann exclaimed.

"Surely you'll let us pay you for the cart," Sarah offered.

"I wouldn't hear of it. It cost me little but time. My sister Christiana was through with the pram, her babes being grown up a bit, and I cadged the scrap iron from the dock," Will explained.

The cart was indeed a welcome addition to the business. Little Johnny took exceptional pride in pushing the machine, as he called it, back and forth to customers, wheeling by the neighbor boys with his chin slightly elevated.

Johnny also took warmly to the machine's "inventor," and Will became a frequent caller. Sarah stayed discreetly in the background, and if she hurt at this additional slight in her loveless life she showed it to neither Ann nor Will.

Ann felt no reticence about discussing Will with Sarah. "He's such a steady man, Sarah. It's different than it was with John Fry."

"He's always there, you mean," Sarah replied, pounding the flat-iron on a stubborn wrinkle.

"It's not only that, his nature is steadier. John was impulsive, never content to be in one place for long. Even when he'd come home, it was only a day or two before he'd start talking about the next voyage."

"He's been awfully good for Johnny," Sarah commented.

Ann nodded as she folded the sheet Sarah had finished pummeling with the iron. "Johnny brags about him to the neighbor boys. And he reads to Sarah and Fanny. He never seems to be without a pamphlet or book, and though I'm sure they understand hardly a word, they love the attention."

"It's been months since he brought the cart—do you think he'll propose?"

Ann smiled, and her blue-gray eyes gleamed. "He may need a hint or two, but I think he might."

"If you've set your cap for him, Ann," Sarah declared, "I'd not give tuppence for the remainder of his bachelorhood."

"He's taking us to meet his sister Christiana next week," Ann confided.

"La, and that's a good sign."

The visit to Christiana was not, however, altogether a pleasant one. Will's sister seemed rather cool, her children stand-offish. Exuberant Johnny and pretty Sarah and Fanny found no friends in Christiana's two girls. Christiana evidently felt Ann's position as a laundress rather less than Will was worthy of. She herself had married a bookkeeper with ambitions and fancied herself moving up the social ladder. A laundress for a sister-in-law did not fit in well with her social aspirations.

Nevertheless Will continued calling on Ann. If he regretted the coolness between Christiana and Ann, neither of them spoke of it.

Shortly after their uncomfortable visit with Christiana, Will urged Ann to take a Sunday off and attend services at the Presbyterian church with him. It was a large, gray stone building, solid and old. Will seemed rather off-handed about his religion.

"Are you a regular churchgoer, Will?" Ann was curious.

"I make an appearance now and then," Will admitted, "but I live a good Christian life. Regular churchgoing may be necessary for some, but I've steady habits and feel none the worse for missing a Sunday here and there."

Ann nodded. Her business kept her from regular attendance at her own Methodist worship services. "You're satisfied with your life then, Will Littlefield," she prompted.

"All in all, I'm not complainin'. I've a good steady job, I've put a bit by—built a good life, all things considered."

"And what do you plan for this bit you've put by," Ann smiled directly into Will's blue eyes.

"I'd no particular place for it when I started, but recently I've considered purchasing a bit of property."

Ann's eyes fell. She had hoped for some other answer.

Will smiled. "Would you be interested in seeing it?"

Ann nodded. They walked the few blocks from the church to a small cottage. The area they passed through was in a more pleasant neighborhood than the Fry home. It was neat, clean, the streets less crooked, and many of the homes had small yards. Even an occasional garden could be spotted. It was not a presumptuous area, and certainly not in the same class with the large homes where most of Ann and Sarah's customers lived, but it was pleasing, nevertheless.

The cottage Will stopped at was white, slightly grayed, but comfortable looking. It sat back from the road and even boasted a rosebush on either side of the door and a windowbox with a single bright pink geranium.

"It's lovely, Will," Ann admired. "Will you let it out or live in it yourself?"

"It would hold all five of us, Ann. Will you marry me?"

Astonished, Ann gasped, but recovered quickly. She smiled at Will, searched his face, and read the sincerity in his eyes. "Will, you dear, I've only been waiting for you to ask."

They married in a simple ceremony in the same Presbyterian church they had attended on the Sunday Will proposed. Ann had no particular attachment to the Methodist church, and offered no objection when Will suggested marrying in his own. Religion was important to Ann, but she felt drawn to no particular church. From what she had gleaned in various conversations she found they all promoted one doctrine above another but were never in agreement. Their differences did little to strengthen one's faith. Ann knew God existed, she did what little reading she could out of the Bible, and from her limited store of knowledge felt something lacking in what either the Presbyterians or Methodists taught. She felt a certain laxness in her religious attitude and wanted to give her children more of a religious background, yet hesitated to teach them adherence to a faith she herself had little confidence in. It seemed an unresolvable problem, and one she had pushed to the back of her mind. Daily life had been enough to wrestle with since John's death.

After a brief honeymoon weekend away, Will and Ann, with the children, returned to live in the white cottage in Portsmouth. Sarah kept on in the old Fry place, but she and Ann moved the laundry business to the cottage, and Sarah came daily to continue working with Ann. The cottage was closer to their clients, and Sarah didn't seem to mind. She seemed genuinely happy for Ann.

Will declared there would be no more seven-day work weeks— six days was all they would labor, and they would observe the Sabbath. With the addition of Will's stable income, the pressure on Ann to earn their daily bread let up, though they still needed both incomes in order to keep up payments on the cottage.

The children adjusted with little difficulty to Will as their father. He seemed to treat each fairly, and the girls looked forward especially to the almost nightly treat of Will reading to them. Johnny was less inclined to sit in on these sessions, preferring to play with his small collection of ships.

Nevertheless, there were adjustments to make. One evening while Will read to the girls, Johnny sat on the parlor floor, his ships spread about him. He supposed there was a storm that endangered his ships, and he howled and moaned in imitation of the great winds.

"Johnny, do be quiet," Sarah pleaded. "I can't hear the story."

Will echoed Sarah's sentiments. "Be a good lad, Johnny, keep it down while Fanny and Sarah have their story."

"But it's a great storm I'm in, and I must have the wind," Johnny argued.

"John," Will repeated rather more firmly, "there's time enough for storms when I'm through reading."

Johnny sulked for a moment, then resumed his howling.

"Johnny!" Will barked. "That will be quite enough!"

The sharpness of Will's voice brought Ann from the kitchen. "Why, Will, whatever is the boy doing, that you should speak to him so?"

"Ann, it's nothing serious. Return to the kitchen, and I will take care of it." Will by this time had set aside the book and moved Fanny and Sarah from off his lap.

"Johnny, what is going on here?" Ann turned to her son.

"He won't let me play," Johnny complained.

"Ann—" Will began.

"It's all right, Will, I'll just take John into the kitchen with me." Ann pushed Johnny ahead of her.

"But, Ann," Will called after her. "That settles nothing."

"La, Will, he's only a boy and boys must play. You go on with your reading, and I'll take care of Johnny just fine."

Will dropped the matter for the time, but spoke to Ann that night about it.

"Ann, I can't be a real father to your boy unless you let me act the part. Remove him from all discipline, and you'll have trouble on your hands," Will warned.

Ann studied her husband. Her eyes warmed as she noted the concern in his face. "I'm sorry, Will. You're absolutely right. I've had the full care of the boy for so long, it comes hard to let go."

"You've a husband to lean on now, woman. And I've a strong back," Will encouraged her. "I'm not one to shirk my responsibility now that I've inherited a family."

But strong back or not, there were times when Will came home too exhausted to do much but eat his supper and fall into bed. He alarmed Ann one night by doubling over after he left the table. He grabbed at his stomach and moaned, stumbling toward the bedroom.

"Will, are you ill?" Ann followed him.

"No, no, I'm not sick—just tired."

"It's not tired you are—you're in pain, Will," Ann insisted.

"It's nothing to worry about. I lifted a bit more than my share today, is all."

"I don't like the looks of you. Perhaps you should see a doctor."

"Ann, I know what's wrong—it's a cursed hernia that bothers me now and then. It always eases though."

"Haven't you a belt to wear? We must get you one at once," Ann fussed.

"I've got a belt, Ann, but it's a miserable contraption. The devil himself must have designed it. I'd rather have a spell like this once in a while than wear that cursed thing all the time."

"I suppose you know what's best, Will, but it seems to me a small price to pay to avoid such pain," Ann relented.

"If you had to wear the blamed thing, you'd know what I'm talking about," Will groaned.

"Men," Ann scoffed. "If they had to spend one week in the underpinnings a woman wears, we'd see some mighty quick changes in the fashions."

Though she tried not to badger Will about it, Ann worried about his condition. When the pain was particularly severe, it brought tears to her own eyes, and she pleaded with him often to see a different doctor or ask about a different belt. She ached to help him, but he stubbornly refused to consider consulting another physician. The best she could do was to warm a brick and tuck him tenderly into bed with it when the attacks came.

The early months of their marriage were ones of discovering who they had really married. Ann was pleased to find Will temperate, for the most part, though inclined to be more firm with the children than she was wont to be. They clashed occasionally over discipline problems, with Ann usually stepping between Will and the children to lessen what she considered to be his harshness. For Will's part, he found that Ann had a stubborn streak that often brought them headlong against one another. He spoke to her of it.

"Ann, you're a fine woman. I'd wager there's not many a man has such an energetic wife. Of course, you're a bit headstrong. Don't know if that's the Toomer in you, or if it comes from running your own life while a widow."

"So, I'm a bit headstrong for you. Have you forgotten, Will Littlefield, that before we were married you spoke of that trait as my 'winning way'? Now it's headstrong I've become. Well, I'm not sorry for you. A man that takes twenty years choosing a wife certainly has had time to look the field over, and had better be satisfied with his lot." And she flounced out of the room.

Will smiled, and called after her. "And it's a bit of a temper I see in you, too!"

"Read that part again," Sarah pleaded with Will. "Mum, come hear this."

"Ann, do come and hear this. Mr. Dickens has really outdone himself this time. We're enjoying this so much," Will called to Ann.

Ann joined her family in the parlor. It was a pleasant room. They'd been able to rid themselves of the old battered sofa, and in its place was a real horsehair loveseat with a high, wood-framed back. Ann found it rather stickery to sit on, though, and usually chose a straight-backed rocker.

"Read away, then," Ann called out as she settled down in her chair. "Tell me a bit about what's happening first, though."

"Paul Dombey is a little boy who has been sent away by his father for a proper education," Will explained. "Mrs. Pipchin is his guardian, and she has rather a high opinion of herself, believing she is everything saintly and good in the world. You know the sort—she thinks she's the blue hen's chicken. Actually, she's a self-serving beast of a woman. Paul, being an intelligent lad, has no trouble placing her where she belongs."

Will read from the pamphlet:

> "Berry's very fond of you, ain't she?" Paul once asked Mrs. Pipchin when they were sitting by the fire with the cat.
>
> "Yes," said Mrs. Pipchin.
>
> "Why?" asked Paul.
>
> "Why!" returned the disconcerted old lady. "How can you ask such things, sir! Why are you fond of your sister Florence?"
>
> "Because she's very good," said Paul. "There's nobody like Florence."
>
> "Well!" retorted Mrs. Pipchin, shortly, "and there's nobody like me, I suppose."
>
> "Ain't there really though?" asked Paul, leaning forward in his chair, and looking at her very hard.
>
> "No," said the old lady.
>
> "I am glad of that," observed Paul, rubbing his hands thoughtfully. "That's a very good thing."

Sarah clapped her hands and laughed, delighted. Ann laughed too. "Mr. Dickens surely has a way with him," she agreed.

"It's so good of you to read to the children, Will," Ann stopped to tell him on her way back to the kitchen. "You're a good father."

Will smiled, pleased with the compliment.

"Have you room on your lap for another?"

"Are you thinking of joining us, Ann?"

"Actually, I was thinking more in terms of someone a lot smaller than me."

"Ann, what're you saying?"

"A baby, Will. Come August you'll be a father in your own right."

Will was thrilled. He became quite solicitous of Ann and clucked over her like a mother hen. He admonished Sarah to watch Ann in the laundry that she didn't lift anything too heavy, and when he was home he insisted on lifting and carting for her himself.

In the meantime family and friends began dragging out all the childbirth dos and don'ts. Everyone had advice to offer.

Within a short time of Ann's delivery date, they located a midwife they felt was suitable. She came by to check Ann over.

"My name is Mary Ann Bray." She was a big woman, with bristly wisps of gray hair that persistently escaped the numerous hairpins stuck about on her head, and who tromped rather than walked. Yet her hands when she examined Ann's protruding belly were gentle. She left instructions for Ann, including several that Ann ignored, considering them senseless superstitions. Having been through the process three times previously, she felt she had a pretty good idea of what to do and what to expect. And the delivery itself went smoothly. Will was skittish and nervous, but performed his single task of fetching Mary Ann Bray without losing his way and got her there in time. In fairly short order a blond-haired little girl was placed in Ann's arms.

"We haven't decided on a name, Mary. What do you think?" Ann mused while admiring her new daughter.

"Why, name 'er after me. I brought 'er into the world. And what a good job I done!"

"What do you think, father?" Ann consulted her beaming husband.

"Mary Ann Littlefield has a nice ring to it," Will declared. "Mary Ann it is."

The midwife bent over the tiny bundle. "You didn't wear the garlic like I told you. I do 'ope it won't 'urt 'er none."

They took little Mary Ann to the Presbyterian church to be chris-
tened. Ann had found nothing exceptionally appealing about the
Presbyterians, and felt neither more nor less at home there than she
had with the Methodists. She had questions about either religion—
questions that bothered her, but that she accepted as natural and
probably not her place to get the answers to. She felt that those more
learned than she were more likely to search out those answers, and
she was content with her life as it was. Nevertheless, she was interested when Sarah approached her one day about attending a meeting
she had seen notice of posted in the bakery window.

"Come along, Ann. It's probably nonsense, but it will be fun to
get out. Can you get Will to take us?"

Will was not very interested, but was not opposed to Ann's going
with Sarah to the meeting. And when his hernia acted up again on
the night of the meeting, he offered no objection to their going on
without him.

"What's the name of this here new religion?" Will wanted to
know as Ann left.

"Sarah said they call themselves 'Mormons.' An odd name, don't
you think?"

4

Winter 1847 to Early 1850

What though the world in malice
despise these mighty things

Hymns, no. 182

The young men seemed pleasant enough. Elders Coggle and Willie, as they introduced themselves, were ordinary in appearance and dressed similarly in black suits and top hats. Ann watched them closely. She was not about to be taken in by shysters.

The posters proclaiming the new religion had made some fantastic claims—a prophet, a new Bible, even modern revelation. Ann was interested, but skeptical, and along with Sarah, had attended the meeting more with an eye to getting out for an evening than anything else.

The elders opened the meeting with two songs, the first of which was familiar to the audience, who sang right along. But the second hymn, new to most of the people, forced the elders into a quavering duet.

Ann looked around the small room while the music faltered on. It was longer than it was wide, and featured a small dais at the end opposite the door. Small, heavily curtained windows looked down on a quantity of straight-backed, armless wooden chairs. The air was thick with stale tobacco odors, and several of the congregation were making their own pungent contribution to the heavy atmosphere with either pipes or cigars. Ann was suddenly glad Will had no inclination to smoke.

She coughed discreetly, then turned her attention to Elder Coggle, who began to speak. In a firm voice that carried clearly, he told the strangest story Ann had ever heard. She leaned forward in her seat.

"In a small farming community in the northeastern part of the United States, a young man, a mere fourteen years of age, pondered a serious question. Which of all the churches was right? Reading his Bible one day, he came to James 1:5 . . . " Elder Coggle continued his presentation steadily. He was not a flowery speaker, but rather spoke in almost a matter-of-fact tone, stating what he genuinely believed. He seemed to be making no real effort to persuade, only to tell the story of the new religion and a man called Joseph Smith.

As Ann listened her pulse quickened. She felt a growing excitement that started somewhere in the pit of her stomach and spread rapidly through her veins. She became so caught up in what the minister was saying that she was completely startled when Sarah suddenly gripped her arm. Ann looked quickly at her sister, but Sarah was gazing straight ahead at the speaker. She appeared to be as fascinated as was Ann herself. The two sisters scarcely dared breathe as the story unfolded.

The elder sat down at last, and Elder Willie stepped forward. "I bear humble testimony to you, ladies and gentlemen of Portsmouth, that this man has spoken nothing but truth to you. He is—we are—authorized messengers of the restored gospel, and we have come to share it with all who wish to hear it. After we have a benediction on these proceedings we will be most happy to answer your questions and provide such reading material as you may be interested in obtaining."

Ann and Sarah were not the only ones who hurried forward to take advantage of that offer. Quite a few of the congregation pressed about the two young men for more information. Many purchased copies of the "gold Bible," Ann and Sarah included. Neither had said a word to the other.

Down on the street they turned to each other. Sarah's eyes were alight as Ann studied her face.

"I feel as though I've been grabbed by a terrier and thoroughly shaken," Sarah spoke at last.

Ann laughed, a welcome release from some of the emotion that had engulfed her at the meeting. Evidently Sarah had experienced the same thing. "It's quite a story, isn't it," Ann murmured.

"Ann." Sarah's face grew sober and intent. "It's *true!*"

Ann shivered involuntarily, though it wasn't particularly cold. "Sarah, I've got to hurry home. Will will be worried. Can you get home alone all right?"

Sarah nodded, patted Ann's arm and turned away, walking with measured steps toward her little house. In a few steps her tall figure was swallowed by the gathering fog.

Ann shivered again, wrapped her shawl more closely about her, and finished tying on her bonnet. She hurried home to find an anxious husband.

Will was in the parlor. The candle had burned low, and his paper lay idly in his lap.

"Will, are you still reading?"

"No, I'm not, Ann. I was getting much too worried to read," he answered softly, a trace of irritation in his voice.

"Will, I'm sorry to have worried you. The meeting didn't really take that long, but Sarah and I stopped after to ask some questions."

"Well, I hope you satisfied yourselves concerning this new religion. I found their advertisement here in the paper. They must have been hooted out of the hall."

"Actually, it's quite a story. I wish you could have heard these men yourself. I did bring a copy of that new Bible home though—"

Will cut her off sharply. "You did what?"

"I thought you'd be interested in reading it. I certainly am!"

"Ann, you didn't waste my hard-earned money on rubbish. Surely you put no stock in what these men told you. You've much too much sense for that!"

"Will, dear, don't get so excited. They piqued my curiosity was all, and I saw no harm in getting a copy of the book. What harm could there be in a Bible?"

"For heaven's sake, Ann, don't show that thing to any of our neighbors. They'll think we've gone daft," Will exploded.

Ann studied Will's worried face. She stepped up to him and put her hands on his shoulders. She looked into his eyes, nearly level with her own, and soothed a hand across his temple. "Will, let's not fret about it. It's late. We've both work to attend to tomorrow. We'll go to bed and talk about it some other time."

Will's arms slipped around her. He leaned to kiss her, then smiled. "I'm sorry—there's no need for me to yell at you. You're a sensible woman, Ann Littlefield. Let's put this day to bed."

Ann nodded, yawned sleepily, and walked arm and arm with Will to their bedroom.

After seeing Will off to work the next morning, Ann roused the children, dressed and fed them, and sent John off to school. She bathed little Mary Ann in the great washtub she'd put on to heat for the day's laundry chores, and was just dressing her when Sarah bustled in.

Ann looked twice at her sister. Her hair was tousled, and there were shadows under her eyes, yet her face was so animated her appearance baffled Ann.

"Sarah, whatever—"

"Ann," Sarah cut her off. "I've been up all night reading this book—" She clutched a copy of the Mormon Bible she'd purchased the night before.

"Sarah, you're a sight. Take a few minutes and freshen up. And for heaven's sake, calm yourself. You'll take a fit in such a state."

"Ann, it's so wonderful. Have you read any of it yet? It's much like the Bible, yet it's different. It's true, Ann. I can feel it—I can sense it. Every page of that book tells me it's true. Let me tell you about this one part—"

"Wait—wait. Sarah, slow down. You sound beside yourself." Ann calmed her sister, at least to a degree, and the two women moved quickly into preparing for the day's laundry business. They performed their various chores nearly automatically while they spoke incessantly of the new religion, the Mormons, Elders Coggle and Willie. Ann's own excitement welled up again. Sarah's fervor was quite infectious—or was it something else? During a lull late in the afternoon, while Sarah was out taking down clothes, Ann curled up on the horsehair sofa, ignoring the bristly surface, and began reading the Book of Mormon.

After supper when the children were in bed, Ann returned to her reading.

Will looked up from where he'd settled with his nightly paper and frowned. "Ann, I thought we'd settled this business."

"Nothing was 'settled,' Will, we only agreed to talk another time," Ann spoke quietly.

"You're being taken in by this new notion, and I'll not have it," Will replied firmly.

"It's just so I won't be taken in that I want to read this book. Surely if there is anything false and these men are scalawags, I'll be able to tell from their literature."

"You're not a reader, Ann. Just because it's printed up and published doesn't make it authentic." Will's voice began to betray his irritation.

"I'm not that gullible, Will. I can think and reason. If 'tis false, I'll know."

"What makes you think you're smarter than any other woman? As head of this house, I must have the say as to what goes on here. I forbid your reading that book." Will stood and waggled a finger at Ann.

She drew in a long breath. "Are you telling me that a woman has not the sense to discover falsehood from truth—simply because she's a woman? I've a mind of my own, Will Littlefield. I got along for five years without a man to discover truth for me."

"And I got along for twenty years without a woman to challenge my intelligence," Will fumed.

"I have no desire to challenge you or any other man, Will, but I will not be told what I can or cannot read."

"Why are you suddenly interested in reading? Ann, put the book away and come to bed *now*. And we'll have no more discussion about it." Will's voice was calmer, though no less adamant.

"I'm staying up to read, Will." Ann's eyes flashed and her gaze was unwavering.

He continued to stand for a moment, baffled by his wife's obstinacy. A tumult of emotions ran through him—anger, frustration, a twinge of fear that somehow, through this crazy religion, their way of life might be changed from the steady, comfortable routine into which it had settled. At last he turned abruptly and went into the bedroom.

Ann sighed. She, too, was baffled. Why was Will so dead set against her reading what appeared to be a quite harmless book? Ann had not found it as exciting as Sarah. Its lengthy accounts of war and bloodshed were not to her taste. But there were powerful moments, too, that seemed to speak right to the center of Ann's being. She had intended going to bed when she finished the chapter she was on, but taking advantage of the quiet of the cottage, Ann read on for a while longer.

When she finally did go into the bedroom, Will was stretched out on his side of the large four-poster. Though it was difficult to see by the light of the candle, Ann knew he was still awake. She undressed quickly, slipped into her nightgown, and unpinned her hair and stuffed it into a ruffled cap. The bedsprings protested noisily as Ann lay down, careful not to touch her obviously still angry husband.

Ann sighed once again. Will was usually so good about allowing her to warm her feet against his always toasty legs and feet. But not tonight. Ann drew her knees up within the confines of her nightgown and tucked the hem around her chilled feet. For a time there was only the sound of steady measured breathing. It was a while before they both fell asleep.

Ann arose from her knees and sat for a moment on the edge of the bed, enjoying the peaceful joy that flooded through her. Prayer had never been so satisfying an experience. In accordance with instructions from the two elders, and following the admonition Ann had found at the end of the Book of Mormon, Ann had knelt beside her bed and asked about its truthfulness. Her prayer had not been the usual perfunctory solicitation of blessings, but a simple straightforward question—is it true? The "it" encompassed both the book and the religion. A sweet warmth had run quietly through Ann's veins and filled her with a sure happiness, confirming what Ann had felt at the first meeting. With a grateful heart she looked up, closed her eyes, and uttered her thanks. "My God, I thank you. I thank you with all my soul for this witness." The emotion of the moment welled up within her, filled her eyes beneath their closed lids, and spilled down the corners of both eyes. Even the tears felt warm, and she brushed them away gently, treasuring the completeness of the moment.

Fanny tumbled into the room. "Mum, Johnny's eaten all the mush, and Sarah's combing her hair again and primping and won't help me."

Ann smiled. She brushed back a lock of Fanny's curly black hair and then stood up. Much as Ann would have loved to hang onto that bit of heaven, she knew she had to return to earthly things. Ann took her little worldly ambassador by the hand and walked into the kitchen.

"We'll have more mush cooked in just a wink, Fanny," Ann assured her daughter. "Now, you see that Mary Ann isn't into any mischief."

The day's routine consumed Ann's thoughts, though the peace remained at the core of her heart. Occasionally, though, a twinge of uneasiness jangled at her calm. She and Sarah discussed how Ann could approach her adamant husband.

Will had not been able to dissuade Ann from reading the Book of Mormon, but he was determined that she stop there and not associate herself with the people themselves. "Now then, Ann, you've proved you're an independent soul," he said to her firmly at supper one night shortly after she had completed her reading. "If you have sympathies with these Mormons, so be it, but I'll not have you fraternizing with them."

Ann was surprised at her inward calm. She had accepted the Book of Mormon, the story of the boy prophet, everything she had been taught about this new religion, and she warmed to its message more every day. A small solid core of faith in its truthfulness had rooted itself in her being, and she knew it was there to stay. The knowledge calmed her and soothed her in the face of Will's obstinate objections.

"Dear Will, I love you deeply, and I want so much for you to feel what I feel about this. Can't you try to understand?"

"Understand? It's you who must understand. I've had nothing but misgivings about this whole business. And now at work the men have taken to razzing me. 'Where's yer gold Bible, Littlefield?' 'Got yourself another wife round about, Littlefield?' 'Have you been dunked yet, Littlefield?' I don't like being singled out, Ann, and I won't take much more of it."

"You're my husband, Will, and I recognize your place at the head of this family. That's why I want so badly to have your blessing." Ann looked pleadingly at Will. "Please, I want very much to become a part of this church. I want to be baptized."

"Out of the question, Ann. Absolutely out of the question."

Johnny kept his eyes on his plate while Sarah and Fanny watched first Will, then Ann, as they talked.

"It didn't make a difference that I was a Methodist and you a Presbyterian," Ann said softly.

"The Methodists are a respectable people. These Mormons are apart from decent folk. They turn their noses up at other religions and think they're better than anyone else."

"That simply isn't true, Will. If you'd only turn a deaf ear to the accusations you've heard others make, and come to a meeting or read some of their literature, you'd know for yourself what the Mormons are like."

"May I be excused, Mum?" Johnny asked.

Ann nodded distractedly, but Will barked, "Don't interrupt, John. And sit down and clean up that plate."

"I'm not hungry," John replied a trifle sullenly.

"Do as your father says, John. You are rude to interrupt," Ann agreed.

"He's not my father," John mumbled.

"He's my husband, and you'll act with respect," Ann insisted.

"I'm not really hungry, Mum. Please, could I go out for a while?"

"If your father will excuse you, I've no objections."

John looked expectantly at his stepfather. "Go on, you stubborn pup." Will waved at John. "But mind you're home when the lamplighter goes by."

Ann began scraping dishes and clearing up after their meal. "You're excused, too, girls. Go along with you now."

Sarah untied Mary Ann from the high stool she was propped up on. "Shall I get Mary ready for bed, Mum?"

"There's a dear girl, Sarah. If you will, please." Ann pondered how to soften Will's implacable resistance. She knew she had to be careful. He was obviously irritated, and was coming in for some embarrassing scenes at work. She decided to tread softly for a while, expecting that she could eventually reach him peacefully and avoid an obvious conflict.

But there was conflict, and there seemed to be no immediate resolution. Rather than argue about it, though, Ann left her Book of Mormon conspicuously about, hoping Will would pick it up and read it. Or she'd bring home a tract from a meeting. She and Sarah began walking from Portsmouth to nearby villages to attend the meetings the elders held as they proselyted throughout the area. It began affecting their laundry business. There was a noticeable drop in profits.

Will, too, decided he'd not provoke Ann about the Mormons. He'd let things cool for a while and probably her fascination for these fanatics would fade away without further distress to either of them. He ignored the tracts, the Book of Mormon, and the drop in their income from the occasionally neglected laundry customer.

"I've a half day off tomorrow, Ann. I thought I'd take John to the docks and show him about a bit."

"Oh, Will, that would be good for both of you. I know John would like that. But I worry about filling his head with the glamour of ships and the sea. I've no desire to arouse a desire in him to be a seaman like his father," Ann cautioned.

"Not to worry, woman, it's more the work among the ironmongers I've an eye to showing him," Will assured her.

"There's something else, Will," Ann spoke softly. She paused. "I want to make arrangements to be baptized. And I ask you with all my heart for your blessing."

For a moment Will's eyes grew hard and angry. He stepped toward Ann and fastened his hands on her shoulders. His fingers clamped uncomfortably into her arms. Ann was startled, and looked at him fearfully.

"I can give you no such blessing." Will spoke in biting tones. He dropped his hands to his sides. "I can't tie you down and lock you in the house. And I don't want to make more of this than it warrants, so I won't forbid you. But there is one promise that I must insist upon—I don't want my children mixed up in this. Promise that and I'll not stand in the way of your baptism."

It's the best way, Will thought. *With that stubborn streak of hers she'd only fight back harder if I oppose her. This notion will burn itself out.*

Ann breathed a sigh of relief. He was relenting. She was sure it was only a matter of time before he softened up and took an interest in the Church in his own right, and then there would be no problem with the children following their lead. "Thank you, Will. It's good to be able to come to a middle road about this."

Will nodded with a short quick movement and turned away. Ann packed her husband's lunch with a cold meat pie and tea. In the bottom of a narrow cylindrical metal container she first laid a few small glowing coals from the cooking fire. Into a small tin with its own lid that fit snugly inside the cylinder Ann poured a generous portion of strong black tea. The meat pie was placed atop that, and in a sudden swelling of gratitude for her husband's compromise, Ann tucked in a sweet treat also. She closed up the whole cylinder with a screw-on lid. Will tucked it under his arm, kissed Ann briefly on the cheek, and strode off toward the dockyards.

When Sarah arrived for their laundry work that day, Ann was ecstatic. "Tomorrow, Sarah," Ann exclaimed. "Tomorrow we can be baptized!"

"Ann, how did you get Will to agree?" Sarah exclaimed. They hugged in shared joy.

"Will doesn't exactly agree—he just said he'd not stand in my way," Ann confided. "But I'm not to involve the children."

Sarah's eyes clouded, and a frown appeared between her dark brows. "Is that a promise you can keep?"

"La, Sarah, if Will is beginning to give in already, it won't be too long before we get him to come round altogether," Ann assured her.

"I suppose you know Will better than I, Ann, but—"

"I'm usually the worrier, Sarah. I'm sure it will all work out."

On a cool mid-October day, Ann Toomer Fry Littlefield was baptized. In spite of her wet clothes, a familiar comforting warmth filled Ann and sang through her veins. The rightness of this hard-won step filled her heart and steeled her. It was a strength she was to need in a fairly short time.

The elders spoke briefly at the confirmation services at their next meeting.

"It's the duty of all who have been enlightened and uplifted by the truth, all who have accepted the warning, to warn their neighbors. Do not sit back and think your final step has been taken. Only a mighty army of the righteous will succeed in covering the earth with the message of truth," they exhorted.

Several tracts were available in quantities, and Ann and Sarah gladly took a few and began tucking them into the neatly folded and ironed clothes. They were hurt and dismayed when one by one they lost nearly every customer. In spite of repeated warnings from Will that their income was so low they lacked sufficient funds for the cottage payment, Ann continued with her proselyting zeal.

"Ann, you've got to stop this Mormon nonsense. You can see where it's leading."

"Will, surely this is only temporary—"

"Temporary! You've driven off every one of your customers. The word is out, Ann. You and Sarah will get no more business from this neighborhood. People want nothing to do with you."

"Perhaps there is something else we can do—" Ann countered.

"Don't you understand? It isn't your work—it's your blasted religion! No one wants anything to do with gold diggers and visions and such nonsense." Will tried desperately to make Ann see the futility of it.

"But it's true—I know it's true! I want so much for others to know, too!" Ann was close to tears.

"Now the neighbors are putting their noses in. Old Farthingham down the street cackled at me the other day about getting a bigger place to house my harem. Impersome codger," Will sputtered angrily.

"How sad," Ann lamented. "The truth is so plain, so beautiful, yet they refuse to see it!"

"There's one truth you've yet to accept, Ann, and that's the fact we can no longer keep the cottage. We've missed the last payment, and I've been told to vacate."

"Oh, Will, no!"

"Oh, yes! The man who holds our mortgage won't trust men with Mormon wives either."

Within a week's time their belongings were packed and ready to move. The little cottage was no longer theirs.

5

May to September 1853

And people shall be heard in distant lands
to say, We'll now go up and serve the Lord

Hymns, no. 62

Ann leaned for a moment against the dark red brick of the building and waited for the churning in her stomach to subside. She breathed in deeply of the salty morning air and exhaled slowly. She looked wearily around at the cluttered yard—actually a narrow alley between two tall buildings. A series of clotheslines stitched the structures loosely together.

As the nausea became manageable, Ann hefted the basket of heavy, wet clothes and moved under the first of the empty lines to begin pinning the sodden pieces to the sagging cords. There was no longer any doubt. Ann was pregnant with her seventh child.

She sighed and began figuring the probable birthdate. December, she decided—perhaps before Christmas. The thought brought little immediate joy to Ann's heart. She knew she'd adjust to another child—even rejoice when it arrived, but for now, it was a struggle to reconcile herself to the thought of another mouth to feed. But they would manage. Somehow they always managed.

Ann fastened the last pair of socks to the line with a final pin and dragged the empty basket behind her down the stairs to the basement flat. It had been lonely without Sarah's help to keep at the laundry work. But there was not enough business for the two of them. Sarah had had to take other employment.

Ann closed the door and surveyed the dark room. The only window in the parlor was a mere slit in the wall close to the ceiling at ground level. The walls seemed to give off an ever-present damp mustiness. Ann moved quickly into the kitchen. It was a somewhat cheerier room. One of Ann's laundry customers had given her a discarded pair of bright yellow chintz curtains, and though they were much too large for the high, narrow window, it too at ground level, Ann had hung them happily, pretending the window behind them was much larger, glad for the spot of color they provided. Her eyes were often drawn to them. They reminded her of the large sunny window she had had in her first little house when she had been Ann Fry.

John had left for school. Mary Ann wiped mush from Lydia's face, evidence of the two-year-old's efforts to feed herself.

"No, no, David," Mary Ann was saying. "That's Lydia's milk. You've already had yours."

Ann wished she could buy more milk to give the children. They loved it so. But there was only enough for a small cup each day for each of the two youngest.

It was Friday, and Will would be home at noon. His work schedule had been cut by half for the past week, and he was not likely to be in a good mood. Ann was right. He wasn't.

His greeting to the children was kind enough, but to Ann he spoke curtly.

"A cuppa, if you please, Ann."

She pulled down the tea tin and then looked closely at her husband. "Will, 'tis that hernia acting up again," she sympathized.

"That, and more of the same at the docks. They never seem to tire of dragging up my Mormon wife," he replied wearily.

"I'm so sorry that the men can't leave it alone."

"Well, it's time I did something to convince you you're wrong to divide the family on this matter."

Ann poured the tea into Will's cup. "How can I ever convince you of the truth," Ann countered. "I don't want us to be split on this matter. But you refuse—"

"And I'll continue to refuse until you come to your senses."

Ann sighed and felt the sting of tears behind her eyes. Her pregnancy and Will's unrelenting attacks threatened to destroy her resolve to stay calm. The scene was the same one they had rehearsed frequently, with little or no variation, since they'd moved to the flat

36

three years before. Often they wound up shouting at one another, though Will tried to avoid loud arguments, reluctant to air their problems before the neighbors, and though Ann struggled to remain reasonable and loving. But the arguments eventually erupted anyway, though they never led anywhere nor resolved anything. Will threatened and pounded the table, and Ann became increasingly fearful his anger would become physical and he'd take to beating her, as many husbands did to keep wayward wives obedient. But so far the conflict had been limited to verbal battles.

"I'll tell you one thing, wife of mine, you can just give up trying to get me into that bloody religion of yours. Leave off your hints and bringing home your ministers and those papers you're forever putting in front of my nose—or I'll—I'll—" he fumed.

"Oh, Will, can't you leave off the threats," Ann replied wearily.

"By thunder, I'm through with threats. You'll soon find out—" Will stood suddenly, his chair clattering to the floor.

But a knock on the door abruptly cut off the argument. Mary Ann's voice called joyfully from the parlor. "It's Aunt Sarah, Mum."

Ann sighed with relief. Will never argued in front of Sarah or anyone else. No one else except Ann had ever seen the frightening rages that Will could work himself into. To all outward appearances Will was a dutiful husband and father. Neighbors who heard their occasional loud arguments thought little of it. Any husband worth his salt had the right to keep his family in line. But with visitors, Will was always civil, even pleasant, and Sarah was no exception.

Ann hurried to greet her sister. They exchanged hugs, and Ann drew off Sarah's cape while she untied her own bonnet.

As John and Sarah Jane had done when they were little, the children crowded around their aunt's skirts. She hugged each of them, then led them all to a chair where she sat, pulling two-year-old Lydia up on her lap. David promptly flung himself over the leg Sarah extended for a "horsey" ride. In a moment both little ones were giggling in glee while Mary Ann watched wistfully, too old for such games.

"I've brought you a bit of sugar, Ann," Sarah called out over the children's merriment.

"Soor, Sarah, you're just in time. I'm scraping the bottom of the tin now."

"The lady I clean for fancies herself a generous woman now and again. I'm happy to share with you."

Ann sat across from Sarah and enjoyed her children's laughter.

"I'll come by and help you with the children for meeting on Sunday if you've a mind," Sarah offered.

Ann nodded. "I don't know what I'd do without your help, Sarah."

Sarah looked quickly at Ann and seemed about to say something, then checked herself.

Will emerged from the kitchen with a cup of tea in his hand. He took it over to his sister-in-law.

"How are you, Sarah? What news of James and his family?" Will spoke hospitably, no trace of his anger evident.

Ann's tension eased. At moments like this she could forget the differences between Will and herself—even feel content. Will was a friendly, gracious man. He was invariably kind to guests, and generous with whatever they had. He had even given the elders shelter for the night, and occasionally a meal when they were in need. For the hundredth time Ann recounted the many good qualities she saw in her husband—his steadiness, temperate ways, the way he'd taken in the Fry children and treated them as his own. Maybe Ann was asking too much that they share the same religion. She pondered for a moment while Sarah and Will chatted amiably. Was she wrong to be so strong for the Church? Didn't a wife owe her husband obedience, and loyalty? Was Will right—was it wrong of Ann to bring such division to the family?

She had heard it preached at meeting that wives should honor their husbands, but never follow them into unrighteousness. Will was a good man, but he refused to listen and hardened his heart against the Church. Was refusal to accept the Church and the gospel considered unrighteousness? Ann was bothered with questions and doubts. The Church was true, that was bedrock conviction within her, but outside that she wavered in her relationship to Will. At times she loved him so deeply she felt guilty because others ridiculed him about the Church and her membership in it. Then on times like that following Sunday he would do his best to humiliate and hurt her, and she would ache with frustration.

Will had not said a word about her going to church that day. He'd read his paper, picked up his latest installment of *Bleak House*, and generally remained rather quiet. Getting ready for church could often be an uneasy experience, and they had had frightful arguments at such times, but that day all had gone smoothly right through Sarah's arrival and the family's noisy departure.

In the meeting of the small Portsmouth branch Elder Brown called them to an opening prayer and began speaking on a familiar theme. The Saints continued to be exhorted to emigrate to Zion, the gathering place in America. Every year a large number of fellow members left the small branch and joined with Saints from all over England, and Europe as well, to undertake the long journey to the valley of the Great Salt Lake.

More was involved than mere encouragement or passive mention of the subject in meetings now and then. The gathering was preached at every meeting, mentioned in every casual conversation, until no Latter-day Saint felt fully at ease in remaining on his native soil. Indeed, that very Sunday a message from the *Millennial Star* quoting the Prophet Brigham Young had been read:

> Our mission is not to build up the wicked anywhere. We are called out of the world to build up the kingdom of God. We are here to promote the principles of heaven, and advance the purposes of the Almighty, and no others; and when you spend a dollar to build up any other power or kingdom than Zion which God has established, you are doing wrong, and you will find it out sooner or later.

As always, Ann's heart leaped within her at the thought—Zion! To be surrounded with fellow Saints, to worship freely, to be part of the great gathering predicted for the latter days—Ann longed with all her heart to comply with the counsel of the prophet. Hadn't President Young said it was wrong to stay in England? But it was utterly hopeless. Will could hardly tolerate Ann's travel to Sunday meetings—and America? It was a lovely, but impossible dream.

Suddenly Ann was roused from her thoughts by a loud disturbance.

"I'll have my wife! Yes, my wife! And my children too!"

Ann stiffened in her seat. It was Will's voice. He had done this before—several times. It kept Ann on edge, never knowing when to expect him. Sometimes he'd come after her three or four weeks in a row, then leave off for a while. Just when Ann began to relax at meetings he'd appear again, rudely and loudly demanding that his wife and children return home with him.

Ann, anxious to shorten the embarrassing scene as much as possible, always got up promptly and left. Mortified, her face flushed with humiliation, Ann, as always, arose and turned to gather the children.

But this time the usually silent presiding elder spoke up.

"Sister Littlefield, be seated. We'll put an end to these interruptions once and for all."

Will stopped in confusion. He'd never been challenged before. An elder at the door motioned for a bobby who had been alerted against just such a possibility. The policeman entered and, when apprised of the situation, strode purposefully up the aisle toward Will. Taking Will firmly by the elbow, he steered him back toward the door. " 'Ere now, sir, we'll 'ave none o' that. These folks 'ave the right to meet wi'out the likes o' you descendin' on 'em. They may be a peculiar lot, but they got their rights, same as you 'n me."

Will's face turned a dark red, and he shook his arm free of the policeman's hand. He glared at Ann and the policeman both but spoke not a word, then turned abruptly and stalked out of the room.

Ann buried her face in her hands. Though still deeply embarrassed, she sensed the sympathy of the congregation and their approval of the elder's actions. An elderly woman next to her patted her hand and smiled.

Once at home, though, the relief and shared support of her fellow branch members was missing, and Ann was left alone to face Will's anger. He wasted no time.

"So, you think you've won now that you've got your ministers to sic the police after me?"

"What is it, Mum?" Johnny came in at the sound of Will's angry voice.

"It's nothing, John. Take the children, and help Sarah Jane put them down to a nap," Ann instructed.

"Yes, leave us be, John," Will barked.

John glared at his stepfather but obediently herded the children to their room.

"Will, I did not fetch the police, nor did I ask Elder Brown to do so," Ann said firmly.

"No matter, Ann. I told you before, the time for threats is over. You won't have to worry anymore about me fetching you home from your infernal meetings. Because you won't be there," Will said coolly.

Ann looked at him closely. Will knew he couldn't keep her from the Church. What did he have in mind now?

"You're going to be busy, Ann—busy earning the money to feed and clothe this family. I'm through supporting your fancy notions. I'll pay the rent, but beyond that you'll not get a farthing from my wages."

Ann had never seen such cool, controlled anger in Will before. He seemed so calm on the surface, yet underneath he seethed. She gestured helplessly.

"You have no one to blame but yourself. You're deaf to my pleas. Let's see if the cries of your hungry children have any effect."

"Will, please don't do this! I'm to bear another child—how can I take on this additional burden now?"

John reappeared from the bedroom.

"I told you to leave us be," Will growled angrily.

"I've a right to see to my mother," John retorted.

"You've only what rights I give you, and I say to leave us alone."

"I'm all right, John—for now. What I'll do when this new babe arrives, I don't know. Your stepfather is withdrawing his support of us." Ann's voice faltered and broke.

John stared at Will. At fourteen he was nearly full grown, lean and lanky like his father and a full head taller than Will. "You took your pleasure in making the child. If you were any kind of a father, you'd do your share to feed it."

Ann gasped. "John, that's no way—"

But Will was faster. In a furious release of pent-up anger and spontaneous reaction, he lashed out with his arm and cracked John in the face with the back of his hand.

Sudden tears darted to John's eyes, and he fought them back as his hand rose to his stinging cheek. He ran to the parlor door, flung it wide, and ran out, leaving it open behind him.

"Now then," Will spoke hoarsely. "We'll have an end to this family's rebellion—one way or another." He, too, stormed from the house.

Ann ran to the parlor door. She stared into the gathering gloom of dusk and fog. She didn't know whom to call to—her angry son or her even angrier husband. Helplessly she closed the door and leaned against it. When the tears finally came she welcomed them, collapsing on the floor in a dismal heap.

Sarah listened patiently, her expressive face registering in turn shock, alarm, and sympathy. "Ann, Ann, whatever will you do?"

Ann shook her head slowly. "What else can I do but work to feed us." The tears rolled slowly down her cheeks.

"You'll not leave the Church," Sarah stated, but with a slight question in her voice.

"Heaven knows I don't want to, Sarah, but how much longer can I go on?"

"Remember the Saints in America, Ann. They suffered long and intensively for the Church. And it's still not easy. We can do no less than to carry what we are called upon to bear, whatever it may be."

"Don't you think I've told myself that? And prayed for the strength to do it? But I just don't know—one thing I *do* know, though. It's easier knowing you're with me, Sarah. You always seem to bring me through." Ann smiled briefly.

"Oh Ann," Sarah wailed. "Don't say that—"

Ann looked carefully at her sister. A sudden lurch in the pit of her stomach told her that something was wrong. "What is it—tell me, Sarah!"

"James—and his family—are leaving with the next ship for Zion," Sarah stammered. "And I—" her voice dropped to a whisper, "I'm going with them."

6
December 1853 to Summer 1854

In the furnace God may prove thee

Hymns, no. 212

"Soor, 'ush, Miz' Littlefield, it ain't but a mite more and you'll 'ave yourself another wee 'un, and 'ealthy 'e 'pears to be at that." Mary Ann Bray worked at her midwifery in great earnestness. The big woman cradled the baby's head between her beefy hands and in a moment was cutting the cord and wiping the child carefully. "It's a boy baby, missus, a fittin' Christmas gift for 'is brother Davey."

Ann released her grip on the bedstead. Her hands slowly regained their feeling as the blood resumed its flow. She ached with a bone-crushing weariness. She would have chosen, had there been a choice, a day other than Christmas for the birth of this child.

"What will you be namin' 'im, missus?" Mary Ann Bray needed to know. She didn't seem to feel her job was complete until the child was properly named.

When Ann was properly cared for, Will was summoned to meet his new son. He bent over the bed and examined the bundle in Ann's arms. "He's a fine looking boy, Ann," Will murmured approvingly.

"I'd like to name him Joseph," Ann said softly, "if you've no objections."

"Joseph it will be, Ann," Will agreed. What a paradox the man was. He seemed by nature so cooperative, giving, and loving. Why couldn't it carry through to the Church?

Will paid Mary Ann Bray her fee and nodded as she repeated once again her instructions for mother and child. She never seemed to remember they had been through it all before.

Ann turned to examine young Joseph in more detail. A thick crop of black hair framed the small reddened face. Will returned to admire his son again. Ann's pale face against the pillow while she cradled their son touched him as it never had before. A wave of sympathy washed over him. Ann looked so tired, so worn. She had not wavered in the past few months. Nothing had slowed her down, not her pregnancy, not Sarah's planned departure for America, not the constant struggle to provide food for the family. He loved his wife, but he could not let her throw herself and their family away on the likes of such a religion as she had embraced. There was no use in looking into it as she kept urging him to do. What could there be to a religion that tore its members from their native land and forced them to suffer untold hardships carving out a new existence for themselves? Granted, life was not an easy matter wherever one lived, but didn't a man owe a loyalty to his country, to the earth that had mothered him, and his father, and his father's father, on back till you couldn't count anymore?

Ann watched Will's face as he studied little Joseph. He had a softness in his eyes that she saw too rarely anymore. Maybe now would be a good time to encourage him about the Church.

"You've a special look about you when you see your children for the first time, Will," Ann began.

"They're so tiny, so helpless. It makes a man feel like a giant."

"We've precious little of the world's goods, but we've got a fair crop of nippers," Ann said.

"Do you wonder what they'll come to be?"

"I only pray they'll grow to be God-fearing and work for the kingdom."

"You'll not be preaching at me again, will you?" Will's eyes grew wary.

"Not preaching, Will, only sharing what is precious and true. We could all be sealed up together, for endless time, if you'd only—"

"Stop it, Ann. Can't you get it through your head I'll have nothing to do with your religion? I love England. I was born here, and here I'll die."

"Do you mean that's your only objection to the Church—the call to gather to Zion?" Ann asked with new hope in her heart.

44

"That gathering nonsense is only the least of my objections, Ann. Now, I've no desire to cross swords with you when you've just birthed a child. We'll end this conversation now. I'll be taking my children to Christiana's. That will ease the burden for the older children so's they can better tend you and little Joseph here." He stood up.

"That's sensible, Will." She knew the conversation had better cease there as Will demanded. She sighed, and knew she'd try again some other time, in some other way.

But something new bothered her. She had caught the reference to "my" children. Will seemed to be making a distinction between the children, something he'd never done before. Perhaps he felt if he couldn't persuade his wife, he could at least influence his children.

At any rate, Ann agreed it would be good for Will to visit his sister, particularly since it was Christmas day. He seldom saw her. Christiana had little enough tolerance for a laundress, but a Mormon laundress was more than she could endure. As far as Christiana was concerned, she preferred to pretend Ann didn't exist.

The younger Littlefields found their aunt and her daughters pleasant enough. Certainly the food was more abundant there than they were used to. Christiana made her usual caustic comments, and Will found himself staunchly defending his wife. He knew his wife's faults—her stubbornness, her attachment to a religion that threatened their marriage as well as their very existence, but he did not need his sister to parade them in front of him. There was much to admire and love in Ann, and Will still felt an abundance of both.

"Leave off, Christiana," he instructed his sister. "It's Christmas, and we could ask some peace and goodwill toward one another."

Reluctantly Christiana agreed, and they passed the time more pleasantly. Even the children played together with a fair degree of cordiality. When it came time to return home, Christiana placed a dressed rabbit wrapped in brown paper in Will's hands, instructing him to see that it was fixed for the children. Mary Ann and David thanked their aunt solemnly, and Lydia dipped a little curtsy, saying sweetly, "Thank you, auntie." Christiana laughed and gave her a quick hug.

The rabbit notwithstanding, Ann was slow to recover from Joseph's birth. She had just passed her thirty-fifth birthday, and she simply didn't bounce back as she had been accustomed to doing after childbirth. And the need to earn their food money was still there. Will, in spite of his tenderness with the new baby and a begrudging admiration for Ann's persistence, had not relented either.

Ann gradually returned to working the full day at her laundry. She had been able to accumulate a few customers, none of whom paid very well, and some who employed her services for a time or two, promising payment, and then failed to keep their promises. She tried desperately to keep the children fed, but on some days a thin gruel was all she had to give them. Milk for the youngest was now a thing of the past. Only occasionally could they afford it. Ann nursed young Joseph for as long as she could, knowing he'd get little or no milk when he was weaned. The periods she spent nursing her infant were the only times she rested during the day. In those brief moments of respite her thoughts churned and warred with one another.

Ann fought to contain her panic over Sarah's impending departure. Sarah had been more support to Ann than either of them had realized. Now that she knew Sarah would no longer be there, Ann was frightened at the prospect of standing alone against Will.

Sarah had been at war within herself, too. How could she leave this special sister in the midst of all her trials? She had six children to care for, a husband who stubbornly and cruelly refused to support them, and a seventh child just born. She adored Ann and the children, had felt so much a part of them that it was as though she was leaving half of herself behind with them. Yet Zion beckoned, as though she was a tiny iron filing and Zion was a great magnet, drawing her to it in spite of herself. Yet she was excited about it, too. In spite of the pain of leaving Ann, Sarah was filled with the thrill of the journey itself, happy to be part of such a marvelous undertaking, to travel, to experience some of the vast world only vaguely perceived before.

James and his family were to meet Sarah in Liverpool. Ann took the children to the station to see Sarah off. She tried desperately to find joy in her heart for this opportunity for her sister. Perhaps in Zion Sarah would find a husband and have the children of her own she wanted so much.

"I'm—I'm happy for you, Sarah." Ann smiled tremulously. "I know it's right—it's what has to be."

"Ann, I want so badly to stay here near you. And yet I know I need to be in Zion with the Saints."

"Write to me, Sarah," Ann pleaded. "You know I will miss you—and the children will be anxious to hear from you, too."

Sarah hugged her. Tears started in their eyes. "Ann, hang on. Somehow, it will all work out! It has to. I just know it will."

"You've been the dearest sister anyone could wish for, Sarah. I'll never forget all you've done."

Reluctantly, they parted, and Sarah climbed aboard the train. She hurried to a seat by a window, flung it open, and leaned out. Ann hefted Lydia to her arms, and they waved as the train slowly moved out amid the hissing jets of steam and clang of wheels against the tracks. They waved until they could see each other no longer.

The weather had been threatening for the past couple of days. The skies were gray, and black clouds hovered over the city, reluctant to release their moisture, but reluctant, too, to move on. Ann studied the sky as she dragged the heavy basket of clothes under the lines. Was it or wasn't it going to rain? Did she have time to get these clothes dried or not? Suddenly the decision seemed too much for her as she stared helplessly at the sky.

"I've had enough," she thought to herself. "I can't go on like this much longer. I'll go to Will and tell him he's won—I'll not go back to church." But no sooner had she formed the thoughts in her mind than another voice cried within her. *No! The Church is true! You dare not go back on your covenants.* How often she had heard the elders speak of the sacrifices so many had made—the early apostles, Joseph and Hyrum, thousands in Missouri and Kirtland and Nauvoo. They'd given their lives for Zion. Zion! The city of the pure in heart. Surely it was worth any sacrifice—any trial—any pain and suffering one might imagine.

The clouds hung heavy and black in the sky. An ominous rumble rippled overhead. A strength and tension began stealing back into Ann's limbs. She felt the strength, reveled in it, and turned her face to the sky once again.

Aloud she shouted, "It *is* true, and I shan't give it up. I'll stand true if it takes my life, too!"

And suddenly the clouds parted, rolling away as though pushed with great hands. The sun poured brightly down, its shafts falling squarely on the narrow alley where Ann Littlefield stood shaking her fist at the sky. And in the quiet of her soul a voice spoke. "Greater faith I have not seen in all Israel." Ann's heart swelled within her. The familiar warmth and peace spread rapidly throughout her body, and she knew she would falter no more.

Reluctantly, but with renewed conviction, Ann put Sarah Jane and Fanny out to work. The few pennies they brought home once a week helped, but more than that, it helped to have fewer to feed each day. The girls were used to hard work. They had kept the house, tended the younger children, and had helped Ann with the laundry as often as possible. Ann ached to see them go out to work so young, but she knew there was no choice. Will still would not yield his wages for food and clothes.

Ann's conviction of the truth of the Church steadied and buoyed her up, preventing her from caving in under the burden of feeding and clothing her large family. She seemed to move from one day to the next in an almost unreal existence. She awoke each morning never knowing if she and the children could bring in enough to feed them, always feeling the pangs of hunger, eating bits of food that only seemed to whet the appetite rather than fill their empty stomachs.

Yet still at the center of all her thoughts, her dreams of joining Sarah in Zion, Ann hoped to convert Will. She prayed nightly for him—long prayers, often choked with tears, pleading for the softening of his heart and the yielding of his resolve to block their family's progression in the Church.

There was too much that was good in Will to abandon all hope for his conversion, and Ann felt strongly her marital responsibilities. She saw no other way for her to accomplish her goal of eternal salvation than for Will to be at her side. Yet Will was becoming increasingly distant from her, no matter how she fought against it. Bit by bit, she felt him withdrawing behind a veneer of hardness that was difficult for her to penetrate.

"Read to me, Father," Lydia begged one night at supper.

David and Mary Ann echoed her sentiments. But Will seemed not to have heard.

"There's a bit of cabbage left, John," Ann spoke to her son across the table.

Will picked up the bowl and scraped the cabbage onto Mary Ann's plate. She looked sheepishly at John and began nibbling at it. But suddenly she didn't feel as hungry as she had a moment before.

"That was offered to me," John blurted. "I've had naun but mush this morning, and I'm still hungry." Will offered no comment.

Lydia stepped into the awkward silence. "Will you read to us, Father? It's been a while. Isn't there a new Dickens?"

"Not tonight, Lydia," Will answered.

Ann's eyes misted for a moment. Will seemed to be taking out his frustration on the children. It wasn't enough that they went hungry so much of the time. Now he seemed to want to set them against one another. Perhaps by division he hoped to accomplish what oppression had thus far failed to do. But Ann held her tongue and smothered the ache. In a moment the table was once again bubbling with the children's chatter.

48

Except for John. John's eyes smoldered, and when he saw he'd get no satisfaction from either his stepfather or his mother, he shoved his plate back on the table, muttered a biting request to be excused, and left the kitchen.

Ann was worried about her eldest son. He'd grown sullen and testy, with her as well as with Will. Ann was adamant in her desire to keep John in school as long as possible. He would soon be sixteen and was already murmuring about quitting school—had even, to Ann's horror, mentioned the sea once or twice. His grades were poor, and Ann had gotten more than one letter from the headmaster in the past year warning of John's reluctance to do his schoolwork. Then one day a letter came saying John had been expelled.

He stood with his back to her, hands thrust deep in his pockets, cap cocked, the picture of defiance. Ann wondered where the once sweet, pliable child had gone. Almost overnight Johnny had been transformed from a young colt testing the fence to the spoiled horse.

"Tell me your side, son," Ann spoke quietly. "I want to know what happened."

"Would you really, Mum? You never believed me before. You've never taken my part."

"John, all I've ever wanted for you was to get a good education. With an education you can make something of yourself. Don't you think I could have sent you out to work long before this? Heaven knows we could use the money. But I wanted you to start out with more than your father and I had—"

"I'm sick of it—the books, the sums, the schoolmasters harping at me with no end. It's time I was on my own," Johnny blurted.

"Doing what? Grubbing in the mines, or on the docks?"

"At sea! I'll go to sea. What do I need with booklearning at sea?"

Ann's heart lurched. "You shan't go to sea, John. Never! You're not yet sixteen, and I'll not sign for you."

John stared at his mother, belligerence in every line of his body. They'd gone over this ground before. He couldn't understand her stubbornness. He could be a help to her. He was a man now, should be putting in his share for the family upkeep. He'd love to get away—out to sea, sail on a ship far away from the constant bickering between Will and Ann, away from the hunger, the cries of the younger children when there was not enough food. Why not the sea? They were surrounded by it in Portsmouth. Nearly everyone there had some connection with it. It was a natural way to make a living, and John saw nothing wrong with it.

Ann could see nothing *but* wrong in it. The horror of her first husband's death—his loss at sea—had never entirely left her. It lurked in a corner of her heart and always stabbed at her insides when her son began showing inclinations of following in his father's path. How could she make her son see that the seaman's life was not for him? How could she make him open his eyes and really see the old sailors with empty sleeves and peg legs, evidence of amputations at sea without benefit of anesthetic? How could she make him really hear and understand the fierce storms that seamen endured, and were often lost in, or taste the brackish water, and the scurvy food?

Ann realized they were getting nowhere. She spoke more softly. "John, we'll work this out. Please give us some time. Try to think it through. We both need more time."

After supper that night John left to be with his friends. Ann spoke to Will.

"What will I do with him, Will?" she cried.

Will raised his eyebrows and snorted.

"You ask me that now? If you'd given me a free hand with him when he was younger, you wouldn't have this problem. But no, I had no right. He needed a steady hand—a man's hand—and before it became everlastingly too late, a swift kick to the seat of his pants. Now, Ann, you've got your boy all to yourself. John listens now to neither one of us."

Ann made no reply. The cutting edge of truth hurt. She had made mistakes—she could see that now, and she wanted desperately for Will to help her put things to right, but he divorced himself from the situation, offered her no support at all. Somehow, someone had to have the answer. She needed the answer now, or John would defy her openly and run away to sea, with or without her permission.

Ann took her problem to the Lord. Morning and night she filled her prayers with supplications for wisdom to solve the problem. Will had no answers for her, but she prayed the Lord would.

In the meantime, Will had no thought for easing up on her during this difficult time with John. Even knowing she was nearly eaten up with worry, he still obstinately blocked her every effort to interest him in the Church, still made it as difficult as possible for her to leave the flat for meetings in any semblance of peace or good conscience. The children cringed under their father's harsh discipline. He seemed to come down hardest on the Fry children—though he mostly ignored John. But he could sense that his own four were drawing closer to Ann, could see their growing attachment to Ann's religion.

50

It only made him steel himself all the more. He stewed and schemed and seemed to be angry most of the time. Even when he walked out alone, he talked to himself in angry outbursts and devised insidious plots to thwart Ann's devotion to the Mormon religion. It became particularly severe one Sunday morning.

Ann was dressing Joseph when he came in. "Ah, it's good you're home, Will. I was just about to leave for meeting."

"You'll be taking the children, I suppose," Will spoke in a low voice.

"As I always do," Ann responded, and pulled a pair of booties over young Joseph's feet.

"But not Joey."

"La, and he's no bother. We'll do just fine." Ann smiled at her infant. He was to receive a blessing that morning.

"It's not the bother, and you know it. I am telling you the boy stays."

Ann looked at Will. His face was flushed with a growing irritation.

"What harm can there be in my taking the baby to church with the rest? I've kept him home these many weeks until he's plenty strong enough."

"I'll tell you what harm can be done. He can be turned from me like the other children. Long ago you promised you'd not take the children with you into this fanatic religion of yours. And I said nothing when John, Sarah Jane, and Fanny all followed along. After all, they were not really mine. And I've not raised the issue with Mary Ann or David or Lydia—hoping you'd eventually come to your senses. Do you remember your promise, Ann? Do you?" He was close to shouting.

"Yes, I remember saying something to that effect, but I was sure you would join us by this time."

"Well, I'm finally holding you to your word, Ann. The time of accounting has come. I'm drawing the line. You shan't take Joey and make a Mormon out of him!"

Once again Will's seething, cold anger was just beneath the surface. Ann shivered. She knew argument was of no use. Yet she knew she could not back down either. Joseph must receive his name and blessing and become a part of the Church. She could not allow Will to drive a wedge between her and her son. Without further argument she turned from her husband and went on with her preparations.

Will stood in the doorway. "So you intend to disregard me once again, do you?"

Ann kept her silence.

"Mark my words, Ann, you'll not have your way." Will flung the words at her and then turned and left the room.

Ann hurried along, bundling Joseph in his blanket. She called to the other children. "Get your wraps now, we must hurry."

But Will stood in the doorway once again. He spoke in a low, ominous voice. "Go if you will, but by heaven, Ann, if you pass by me I will cut you both down!" In his hands he gripped an ax, and as he spoke he raised it high above his head.

Ann gasped. She'd always feared there might be violence within her husband. His anger sometimes reached such a pitch she'd felt certain he would lose control one day and strike her to the ground. But an ax! She paused for a moment. Could he really cut them both down—his wife and newborn baby? The moment seemed frozen in time. Will stood firmly in the doorway, ax raised, his eyes flint cold with anger. Ann, with Joseph in her arms, and Mary Ann, David, and Lydia clinging fearfully to her skirts, stood equally as firm. *If it's my life is required, it's my life I'll give,* she thought. Moving forward firmly she strode purposefully to the door. Without a glance at Will, she brushed her husband back from the doorway and moved by, the children trailing after her.

The ax clattered to the floor. As Ann continued her way through the parlor and out the front door, Will, his face ashen, leaned against the doorjamb trembling from head to toe. What lengths this woman had driven him to! He loved her, yet he hated her. *How thin a line there is really, between love and hate,* he thought raggedly. He sank into a chair in the parlor and dropped his head in his hands.

When the fury and frustration seemed to abate somewhat, he stood slowly. He walked woodenly to where the ax lay on the floor, picked it up, and put it away. From a cupboard he got out the candle and matches and placed them on the table against Ann's return home. Then he got his cap from the peg behind the kitchen door and went out to walk.

Ann, too, was shaken by the encounter. She scarcely heard the sermon nor the prayers at the meeting, and left quickly while the amen still hung in the air. She was not usually one to linger after meetings anyway, always anxious to get home to prevent a scene with Will. Too, most of the talk after meetings concerned who would be in the next group leaving for Zion, and Ann could not stand the pain of knowing she'd never see Zion. It was better not to dwell on it.

Mary Ann and David raced on ahead of her as usual. It was deep dusk when they arrived at the flat. They clambered down the steps and tentatively opened the door. It was dark inside. Ann had no idea what to expect. Would Will have reached another fever pitch of anger? Was he waiting here in the gloom to cut them down, having gathered courage and strength during their absence? Ann paused for a moment before entering. But in the last vestiges of light Ann spotted the candle and matches on the table. And she understood. It was a small offering, a tiny ray of hope for their agonized relationship.

She lit the candle and called the children to her. In the soft glow of the flickering light, they knelt to pray.

7

Autumn to December 1854

Glorious things of thee are spoken
Hymns, no. 244

Will and Ann stood outside a large, gray stone building near the docks. It was early in the morning, and thin wisps of fog hung here and there between the ships and dockyards and old waterfront buildings. Will was about to report to work.

"This is it, Ann. The Maritime Office. You should be able to find out what you need to know here." Will indicated the door she was to enter.

"Thank you, Will. I feel I've come to the right decision, don't you?"

Will shrugged his shoulders. "It seems we can't do anything with the boy. Perhaps the military can." He paused for a moment. "I'll be off now to work."

Ann stood looking after him for a moment. He'd been subdued after their confrontation with the ax, though nothing had really changed. She still got no help from him as far as food and clothing money, and Will had always been on the quiet side. But still, something had gone out of him. Was he humbled enough to accept the gospel now? A small stir of hope flurried within her. Perhaps Zion was not so impossible after all.

"Beggin' yer pardon, ma'am, can I 'elp you wit' somethin'?" An old seaman stood before her.

"Thank you, but I think I'm at the right place—the Maritime Office?"

"Right as rain, ma'am. That there's the door up them couple a' steps." He pointed a gnarled finger and grinned a near-toothless grin.

Ann smiled and moved into the building. In a matter of moments she was seated before a clerk in the pension department. After a brief explanation of the purpose of her visit, the clerk directed her to yet another department, this time for survivor benefits.

All in all, the visit took a little over an hour. When Ann was through, John Fry was enrolled in the military academy.

"The military academy?" Johnny shouted.

"Johnny, let me explain."

"What's there to explain? You're farmin' me off to some school where you won't have to bother with me no more."

"John, calm down. If you'd think about it for a moment, you'd see it isn't as bad as you think. Your father's death at sea provided for tuition at the academy when you came of age. I wanted to avoid the academy if I could. You know I have no love for the military, but now it seems to be the best thing for all of us."

"Whose idea was this—Will's?"

"It's entirely mine, John Fry. And you'll hear me out." Ann's temper began to flare. "All expenses at the academy are paid for— room, board, books, everything. It will take some of the edge off things here at home, and you'll still be continuing your education."

"Don't you ever listen to me, Mum? 'Tisn't an education I want! I want to be free of school!"

"John, you'll soon be sixteen. Take advantage of this opportunity to complete your education. Do it for me, if you won't do it for yourself. Then, when you are eighteen—" Ann hesitated.

"When I'm eighteen no one can stop me from going to sea," John finished for her.

Ann nodded slowly. *But I'll fight you to the last breath,* she thought.

John mulled it over in his mind. He twisted his cap in his hands and scratched his head. "All right, Mum, if that's the way it is."

Ann sighed. "It's for the best, John. I know it is."

Within a few days all the arrangements were made. Ann packed up John's few belongings, begged the few shillings for his train fare from Will, and tearfully saw him off at the station. *Were train stations always such sad places,* Ann wondered, recalling Sarah's departure.

Wearily Ann retraced her steps home from the station. When the thought about the academy had popped into her mind, it had seemed the perfect solution, and she felt sure it was the answer to her prayers. It accomplished so many things—it relieved the burden at home, John's education was virtually assured, and John would receive the discipline he needed, discipline that neither Ann nor Will were able to provide. Now with her young son's face swimming before her, she began to have doubts. He was still a boy. What would the military do to him? Ann gnawed at her lower lip in agitation. At length she came to the conclusion that she had done the right thing. It hurt to send John away, but the decision was right. The ache in her heart eased a little, and she turned her thoughts to other matters.

Just as Ann turned the corner near the rooms where the Portsmouth Branch meetings were held, Elder Crawley approached her. He was newly arrived in the branch and went about his duties with a vigor and enthusiasm that were sometimes a little grating.

"Sister Littlefield, odd you should come along now. You've been on my mind all day." He fell into step beside her.

"Oh?" Ann replied. "In what regard?"

"I'd like to speak to you at some length about it. May I call at your home this evening while Mr. Littlefield is at home?"

Ann hesitated. Other elders had been to the house. Will, as he always was with guests, had been civil—even kind. The thought flashed through Ann's mind that perhaps this was a good time for him to call, yet Elder Crawley could be a little abrupt. Perhaps Will's subdued attitude for the past little while might be fertile ground for gospel seed. "Why, of course. I'll expect you at, say, eight o'clock?"

The time agreed upon, Elder Crawley took his leave, and Ann hurried home.

Will seemed neither very excited nor upset about Elder Crawley's expected visit. He merely nodded, and when the visitor arrived, greeted him cordially and invited him in. After a few polite exchanges regarding the weather, Elder Crawley got to the point.

"Mr. Littlefield, we've several elders arriving in the area for next week's conference meetings. Could you possibly put one of them up for a night or two?"

So that was the object of his visit! Ann felt a surge of disappointment flood through her. She had hoped the elder would somehow engage Will in a gospel conversation. She glanced at her husband.

"We share what little we have, sir," Will remarked.

"And your hospitality is much appreciated, to be sure." The elder bowed slightly from the waist. "It is very generous of you."

"Christian duty," Will replied. "We can agree on that much."

"Will you take some refreshment, elder?" Ann offered.

He shook his head. "I'm afraid my stomach has yet to settle after my recent crossing, though it's been over a week. I can eat but little until I'm myself again."

"What you need is some chamomile. It's just the thing for a bilious stomach."

"Please don't bother. I really must be on my way soon. And I'm not sure my stomach complaint is not mixed with a twinge of homesickness."

"La, it must be difficult to leave your family."

"Yes, surely. But I miss the mountains that surround our valley as well." He shook his head and paused for a moment. "What do you know of Zion, Sister Littlefield? I can tell you it's a splendid sight."

"So I've heard tell," Ann murmured.

The elder continued his vivid descriptions of the valley: the mountains; the cold, clear streams; the Great Salt Lake, sitting like a jewel on the valley floor. Ann dared for a moment to picture it all in her mind. Her pulse quickened. Again the thought crossed her mind that Zion might somehow, some way be within their reach. Her heart filled with the desire to see Zion, to reach that promised place, that glorious valley of peace and home of the pure in heart.

Will watched Ann carefully while the elder talked. He scarcely heard the elder's lively, enthusiastic comments. *Of course she would want to go,* Will reminded himself. *I've been a fool not to see she's been harboring such thoughts all along. She will bear careful watching.*

At length the travelogue came to an end. Ann and Will exchanged glances, each hiding their thoughts from the other.

"I'm sorry I've taken up so much of your time. I must take my leave." The elder stood, shook hands with Will, and disappeared into the night.

"Thank you, Will, for offering to house one of the elders," Ann said as she closed the door.

"It's nothing." He shrugged. "But how he does go on about that valley!"

"The valley is more than a spot on the map—more even than home to the Saints."

"Zion! The pure in heart. Nonsense, garbage! How can you put any stock in such talk?"

"Doesn't it intrigue you even a little? Is there anything wrong with a people flocking together to live a dream? To make the dream a reality?"

"I've lived long enough to know that such dreams are only that—illusions, fit only for empty-headed visionaries. The only reality is here and now and what we can accomplish with our own hands. God gave us the rules, Ann. And he has left us to live them. Nothing more is needed."

Ann lowered her eyes and sighed. She was much too weary and emotionally drained to argue. She'd run the gamut of emotions that day—anxiety about John's leaving, a heart filled with hope that the elder would somehow get through to Will, the renewed longing to reach Zion, and now the disappointment that Will's heart was as hardened as ever. She could take no more tonight. Without another word she turned aside, picked up one of the candles, and walked into the bedroom.

Will followed her, silent as well. Rapt once again in their own thoughts, they made ready for bed.

Ann fell to her knees beside the bed. She knew all the reasons she could not hope to reach Zion. Will was as implacable as ever, and she was his wife, the mother of his children. She had hoped with all her heart that Will's quiet mood lately was indicative of a humbling, a softening. Without that opening up to the Spirit, Ann despaired of ever reaching him. And without a total willingness to respond to the Spirit, Will would remain forever outside the embrace of the true gospel, and they would both remain far from Zion.

Ann had recited all the reasons it was impossible over and over. But tonight she knew only one thing—*she wanted to go!* How it could come to pass, by what miracle it might occur, she did not know. She knew only that her heart was filled with the desire to gather with the Saints, and she pleaded with the Lord to grant her this desire. "I don't know how, dear Lord, and I don't even care—but please, please, somehow, take us to Zion!"

Her whispered prayers sent heavenward, Ann crawled into bed. Almost at once she slept and began to dream. She found herself in a lovely forest. The trees were tall and formed a natural canopy overhead. The sun shone through the leaves, dappling the forest floor with patches of light. She walked down a winding path that seemed to stretch out before her without an end. And a man walked down the path toward her. He was tall, dressed in a black suit with a white cravat, and in one hand he held the scriptures. Somehow she knew this man was a prophet of the Lord. She hurried toward him and begged him to be allowed to go to Zion.

The prophet smiled kindly. He took her by the hand and spoke softly. "It's not yet time. There is a work here for you to do. You must wait, for more children are to come to you."

"But how long?" Ann cried. "How long must I wait?"

He smiled once again. "Ten years, my dear. Ten years, and then you shall go to Zion."

Abruptly Ann awoke. She knew she'd been dreaming, but she knew, too, the dream represented a promise. Her heart sang within her. Ten years—a long time, a dreadfully long time—but she too, would go to Zion. She could wait. Zion was worth waiting for. Ann turned on her side and slept peacefully.

Once again, Will and Ann entered an era of uneasy truce in their marriage. They avoided talk of the Church. Will ignored her Sunday trips to meetings, even though many times she had to walk long miles to get to them. Conference sessions were rotated among the many small branches in the Southampton area, sometimes as far away as fifteen and seventeen miles.

Ann tried to be a good wife. She treated her husband with deference, saw to his needs, helped him through his occasional bouts with the hernia problem, mended his clothes. She continued to pray for his conversion, confident now that the Lord would help her with this miracle. Always now at the back of her mind was the dream, the promise that had been made to her. She would leave the weight of the problem with the Lord. Will was her husband. The Lord would work His will on him.

Then one day Will thrust the newspaper in front of Ann. The problem it foreshadowed blotted out everything else.

"I'll wager your Johnny will be growing up mighty fast now."

Ann read the headlines Will pointed out. "Cadets Called to the War Front." Ann sank into a chair. Her eyes devoured the article.

> Due to the urgent need for troops, her Majesty Queen Victoria has issued a call to all cadets in every military academy in England to ready themselves for action in the Crimea.

Ann pressed a hand to her mouth. She couldn't let this happen. "Will, what can I do?"

"What can you do? Ann, you know nothing is to be done. Johnny's a cadet. He is called to serve. He will have to go."

Ann wept. "They can't take him. He's just sixteen. They took his father—they can't take him, too."

"Ann, be reasonable. Johnny's under the Queen's orders. There is nothing you can do."

The next few days dragged by. At any moment Ann expected a letter notifying her of John's removal to the front. She'd filled every possible waking moment with fervent prayers to the Lord. Hadn't he answered her prayers before—hadn't he promised her Zion in ten years even though she still could not envision how it would happen? He could save her boy. He must!

Ann scoured the newspaper each night trying to learn more of the war. The more she read, the more horror stricken she became. The war was being poorly managed. The generals of the army were, for the most part, old men who hadn't seen action in years, if at all.

As Ann delivered her laundry she caught fragments of conversations—bits and pieces that filled her with dread. Lord Raglan, directed to head the campaign, was nearly seventy; the Duke of Cambridge, also a ranking officer, had never been in a battle, let alone led one. The troop ships were grossly overcrowded, and cholera was rife throughout the army. The more Ann heard, the more she pondered her petitions to the Lord. She knew she had to make a decision. Exactly what should she ask the Lord for? At length she realized she had few choices.

"I'd rather see Johnny dead than suffer through this war, Lord. I beg you to save him. Take his life if you have to, or make him physically unfit. Take him or smite him!" she prayed. Still no word came from the academy.

Her vigil finally ended one day as she hung clothes in the alley.

"Beggin' your pardon, ma'am, but is this John Fry's 'ome?" Ann whirled around to see a young man facing her. An uneasy chill ran through her as a scene from long ago seemed to reenact itself.

Without waiting for an answer, he turned and led the way to an ambulance wagon. The young man flung open the rear doors and grabbed one end of a litter, Johnny unconscious upon it. A second young man took the other end of the litter, and together they followed Ann into the basement flat.

Ann looked questioningly at the cadet. "Doctor allows as 'ow John'll need more care than 'e can give 'im at the academy, and we'll be gone to war soon anyways. 'E says to tell you to get lots of liquid down 'im."

"But what's wrong with him? What's happened?"

"I'm sorry, didn't I mention? It's the typhoid 'as got 'im. Typhoid fever."

8

Early 1855 to Autumn 1857

Great deliverance, great deliverance Zion's
King vouchsafes to send

Hymns, no. 273

Ann sponged her son's feverish head. She had just changed his bed linen, and yet the sheets were damp again with his sweat. How long could he go on like this? Already it had been weeks. He had had some relatively calm days, but most of the time he tossed and moaned, tormented with a high fever. His hair came out in clumps, and Ann would not have recognized him had she not known he was her son. His normally lean frame was almost skeletal. She kept him fed with broth and weak tea, trying to replace the fluids he lost through his excessive perspiration. His skin was parchmentlike and waxy looking. Ann was only too aware of her request of the Lord—to make John unfit for service in the war in the Crimea. Now she was alarmed for fear the Lord would take him as well as smite him.

Ann begged for more money from Will to give John better food, to strengthen him. She feared he would die before her eyes unless she could get something more substantial down him than thin potato soup and weak tea. But Will only shrugged and ignored her pleas.

"You wanted him out of the war. You've got your wish and then some. There's naun I can do about it," he answered.

Actually, Will watched Ann carefully. In spite of his seeming in-difference, he noted meticulously every move she made. It had been a year since their last open confrontation over the Church. He suspected she might be concocting some plan to trick his wages out of him, to make him back down on his resolute determination to break her. He found he could be a patient man. He could turn his back on her pleas for help, could ignore the children when they whimpered in the night from hunger. He knew he could come out on top of this struggle by sticking to his guns and not letting anything deter him from his avowed course.

He always watched Ann warily as she said her prayers. No matter how late the hour or how bone-tired she seemed to be, she never failed to get onto her knees. Her prayers were always murmured silently, so Will had no way of knowing for certain what she prayed for, but knowing Ann he was sure she sent heavenward many fervent pleas for John's recovery. Beyond that he had no idea. Did she still pray for her elusive Zion? Will wondered.

Will was right. Ann did pray constantly for John's recovery. As the weeks dragged painfully on, and in spite of the lack of adequate nourishment, John seemed to be making progress. Ann felt sure the Lord would have taken him before this if that was His desire.

And Ann continued to pray for Zion as well. She clung to the promise in the dream. A year had passed since she had dreamed it, yet it was never far from her mind.

Mechanically she kept at her laundry work. Sarah Jane and Fanny came by as often as their employers permitted to leave their few pennies with her and to look in on John. At nearly sixteen Sarah Jane was approaching womanhood. She was somewhat on the plain side, but pleasing nevertheless. Fanny's dark good looks were showing signs of maturity too. At thirteen she looked older than her age. Her dark eyes danced as she talked. In spite of Sarah Jane's being named for Ann's sister, it was Fanny who reminded Ann of Sarah. Impulsive, always eager, and outspoken, Fanny had not yet been curbed by life. She was frequently in trouble with her employers because she found it hard to hold her tongue. Yet she was not a flighty child, just given to speaking her mind, the devil take the hindmost.

It was Fanny who called to her mother during one visit. "Mum, come quick. John knows me!"

Ann rushed to the cot she kept in the kitchen. Fanny had been sitting next to her brother, just holding his hand and talking softly to him though she was sure he didn't even know she was there. But gradually Fanny had become aware that John was looking at her— really looking, not staring vacantly as he had done before. His eyes followed her every movement. She was certain he was aware of her presence.

Ann knelt by the cot. She took John's hand in her own and searched his face. His eyes moved from Fanny to his mother.

"Johnny—son—can you really hear me?" Ann's voice quavered.

A tiny smile played around John's lips, and Ann felt a slight squeeze of John's hand on her own.

"Fanny, you're right! He is conscious! The fever seems to have broken at last."

"Rabbits, John, you've given us all quite a turn." She spoke lightly, but tears glistened in her eyes.

Ann dropped her head to the cot. The worst was over.

Ann returned to her work, her heart lighter than it had been in weeks. How grateful she was that the Lord had heard her prayers— had answered them, not once, but over and over again whenever she cried out to him in her need.

John's recovery was slow, but steady. Ann kept his cot in the kitchen, where she spent most of her time. With the fever broken, the broth she fed him began nourishing him. She started him back on solids gradually, sensing more than knowing that he couldn't handle anything more in his weakened condition. She scrimped and cut corners wherever possible to get eggs and milk to make him custards, and if she was able to make a custard a week, she counted herself lucky.

John watched her every move from the cot. Strange he'd never really noticed his mother's constant activity before. She never seemed to be still. If there wasn't a bucking in the huge tub to scrub on the board, there was laundry to hang, or to gather in, or to iron. Or there were Joseph's nappies to change, or the next meal to get ready. More than once he was moved to tears at her constant devotion to him and the others. His rebellion seemed to have burned itself out with the fever, and in its place grew an appreciation for the woman he called mother—and a resolve to make up to her all the grief he had caused.

Will noticed the change in him, too. "He's a different lad, that's for certain," he mentioned to Ann one night.

"He's grown up, that's all. My John's become a man." At least, she thought, he showed all the signs of a new maturity. He was polite and grateful. He spoke respectfully to Ann, and to Will, too. His belligerence had been replaced with a calmness and steadiness Ann rejoiced in.

As John's strength returned, he began moving about. At first, he was as weak as a newborn baby, but gradually his long-dormant muscles tightened and regained their usefulness. He began helping around the house, even took his turn with Joseph's soiled nappies. When he could heft the heavy laundry basket out to the lines for his mother, Ann knew he was at last free of the illness. She encouraged him to get out in the air.

"John, walk a little. The salt air is said to do wonders for convalescents. Get out of this basement and away from this musty air."

He took her advice. Though she worried when he began staying out longer and longer, he seemed to be so much better day by day that she said nothing about her fears.

John's forays into the city had a purpose behind them, a vow he'd made while he still lay weak on the cot and watched his mother work the day, and much of the night, away.

"I'll be needin' a lunch tomorrow, Mum!" he announced on his return from an outing one day. Ann looked at him, a question in her raised eyebrows. "I've got me a job at Sable's Dry Goods. You're looking at his new clerk."

"Oh, Johnny, it's that proud I am of you!" and Ann hugged him to her. He was as tall as his father had been, Ann noted as she looked up into his eyes.

Ann rejoiced even more when she realized John had other plans as well. Regularly he began bringing his wages home to her. "You let up some on that laundry now, Mum!"

Ann welcomed the help. But that was not all. "I'll get you to Zion, Mum. You'll see." Ann's heart leaped within her. Was this the reason John had been spared? Was the Lord working through John to keep His promise to her?

But gradually Ann realized she had other priorities. As the months rolled on and John's bit of savings grew, another plan grew in Ann's head. Sarah Jane and Fanny—she must get them to Zion soon. They were both approaching marriageable age. How could she keep them here with her until Will relented? More children were to come to them, the prophet had told her in the dream. How many more she had no idea, but she knew the ten years were still a long way from being fulfilled. By then it might be too late for her girls. She wanted to spare them the anguish of marrying outside the Church. She must get them to Zion where they could marry fellow Saints. She spoke to John of her fears.

"It's the girls I worry about, John. I know you've saved to get us to

Zion. But believe me, I know the Lord will provide the way in his own due time."

"But Mum, I *want* to do this for you. You must use that money for your passage."

"It's not time for us yet, John. I've the children to see to, and Will to contend with. Somehow the time is not yet right. But *you* go—and take the girls. Take Sarah Jane and Fanny to Zion. The rest will come with time."

Will gradually became aware of their plans. He brooded over it, mulled it over in his mind, trying to figure what it might mean to Ann.

"Now that you've got John's help, Ann, are you throwing it away for such a pipe dream?"

"He's got to have a chance at his own life, Will. I cannot keep him working to support me and the children for all his young life. And I want the girls to have their chance, too."

"Have you no concern to be sending the three of them off halfway around the world?"

"Of course, I'm concerned. I die a thousand times every time I think of sending them off, knowing I may never see them again."

"*May* never see them again? You can be *certain* of it, Ann."

"Be that as it may, it's time to cut them loose, and if it's Zion they want, I'll turn every stone to get them there."

"And what of *my* children? The Fry children are one thing, but me and mine will never leave England."

"I'm aware of your feelings, Will. We needn't quarrel about it."

"You've been aware of my feelings all along, yet it doesn't stop you from doing whatever you want."

"What I want is for you to turn away from your stubborn intentions and let the Spirit teach you of the restored Church."

"Restored church? Restored from what? Restored to what? Why do you insist on blindly following after a religion that flaunts every old tradition in a man's face? What's wrong with the way things were? That's the way I want things, and that's the way I'll have them," he shouted.

"And why do you blindly resist the truth? All you do is object and resist and turn your back. What is it that is so frightening about the Church that it makes you so insensitive?"

"It isn't I who have become the insensitive one. It was you who turned your back on me—me, your husband, the one you promised to *obey*."

"Is that what it is? I've been an obedient wife, Will. In everything you've required of me—except for the Church. I fear for my eternal soul should I refuse to acknowledge the truth and live the gospel. But in all else, you have no reason to fault me."

"I only know I'm the butt of jokes at work, the object of sneers and sniggers from our neighbors, and some sort of a monster in my children's eyes, all because of your insistence on following some fool religion that will burn itself out as soon as this ridiculous proselytizing zeal ends." Will's voice became louder and more strident. "Just know this—you'll never see that Zion of yours, you nor our children either. Just try to take—or send—them there, and I'll see you dead!"

The old fear gripped Ann. Will had been so resigned, so calm, for the past couple of years. Now their uneasy truce had shattered once again.

But drawing strength from an inner resource that always seemed to be there, Ann put her fears aside and moved ahead with her plans. She began putting Sarah Jane's and Fanny's money away for them with John's. She spoke to them as often as possible about Zion, firing them with enthusiasm, encouraging them to work hard for this chance. John worked steadily, and bit by bit the money in the tin grew. Ann kept out only what she absolutely needed to feed the family. They were used to a meager diet, and she allowed no luxuries. It was difficult, knowing the tin was fat with money and could buy a few niceties, but Ann's resolve was strong. It was Zion for her three children—and as soon as possible.

When she once again realized she was pregnant, Ann this time rejoiced from the beginning. At last the children promised to her in the dream were on their way. The pregnancy was a difficult one. Ann refused to slow down her work, and she often felt she would simply drop in her tracks, but she knew she had to keep going. But by the time she was in her seventh month she felt instinctively there was something different about this pregnancy. She called Mary Ann Bray in to check her over.

"Blimey, I'm sure," the midwife exclaimed as she felt Ann's protruding belly.

"Whatever is it, Mrs. Bray?" cried Ann in alarm.

"I'm not sure, but you've either got a wallopin' big 'un there, or twins, unless I miss my guess."

"Twins!" Ann gasped. "Twins?" And then she smiled. The Lord was hurrying things along at last. Ann hadn't many more childbearing years left.

"You can smile, woman? Do you know what you're in for?" Mrs. Bray asked in surprise.

"Whatever it is, I can handle it," Ann replied calmly.

"Well, you've got to get off your feet more. If you want to carry these wee 'uns to term, you need to take it easy."

"I'm sure I'll manage, Mrs. Bray. I'll be calling you when it's time."

Will was shocked, then proud of himself. Twins! They were a rare experience.

"But I've got to have some help, Will. I'll lose them both unless I can let up some with the work."

Will pursed his lips. His eyes narrowed. "This wouldn't be a trick to get my wages, now would it, Ann?"

She couldn't believe her ears. Her temper flared.

"Forget your wages," Ann flung at him. "I'll get through this like I've done everything else—without your help."

How could he think she was trying to trick him? Reluctantly, she dipped into the money tin. She forced herself to lie down for short spells during the day and tried to retire earlier at night. She was cautious in lifting and even asked help from passersby off the street when she had to carry a heavy basket. Somehow the weeks passed. Will watched her warily and offered little help. Actually, his hernia was a frequent problem, and he was little better off than Ann.

By the time she was due she could hardly move around. She prayed for an early delivery—if the children could be born healthy. Early on a May morning she roused Will. "Fetch Mrs. Bray, my water's broke."

"It's a rare privilege, missus, to be birthin' twins," Mary Ann Bray prattled as she worked. "Push now, missus." Ann pushed with all her might, her hands white to the knuckles as she gripped the bedstead above her. The labor went slowly, but eventually with Mrs. Bray's constant encouragement and instruction, Elijah Littlefield made his way into the world. He was followed shortly by Emily Ann.

"Joey, don't poke at the baby's eyes!" Mary Ann led her little brother away from the cradle. David and Lydia were staunch helpers with the twins, but Joseph at age three and a half could hardly contain his curiosity. He was constantly poking and prodding them, laughing gleefully when they screwed up their little mouths and cried. He was fascinated with every aspect of the tiny creatures, and would sit for the longest time just holding onto one of their little fingers. "Yija and Em," as he called them, filled his days with great fun.

They filled his mother's and sisters' days with a constant wariness for fear Joey would accidentally hurt one of the babies with his unbridled curiosity.

Will rarely picked up the babies. His hernia kept him in nearly constant pain now. He often asked one of the other men at work to carry for him, and feared he'd lose his job if things got much worse. He brooded over the situation frequently. Something had to be done. He couldn't continue on this way. He worried about Ann and her zeal for Zion, he worried about the Fry children leaving for America and then their constant pull toward Ann, and he worried about finding other work—work that he could do without aggravating the blasted hernia he suffered with so often.

Ann once again took up the thread of her life. She worked as hard as she possibly could to replace the savings she'd had to dip into to assure the twins' safe arrival. At length, with John's steady contributions and Sarah Jane and Fanny also adding to it, the fund fattened once again. By late summer in 1857 they could see they'd have sufficient money to send the three of them off with the first boatload of Saints to leave England in the spring of 1858. Ann wrote to Sarah in the Salt Lake Valley, warning her they would be coming. Sarah's reply came as quickly as mail could travel.

Dearest Ann:

With what joy I received the latest news I cannot begin to tell you. To think I will again see the dear children I loved as my own fills me beyond expression. Only news that you would be arriving with them could make me any happier.

You left much unsaid in your letter, but I take it that Will has not relented in his unhappy stance. I grieve for you and can only pray that somehow, someday the way will open for you to make your way to our happy Zion.

We have much to do here to bring about the perfection required of those who would inhabit the pure society, as President Young reminds us constantly, yet we feel to rejoice in our blessings and continue to work toward that perfect end.

Hug my dear children—alas, they must be full grown by this time, but children they remain to me. Until a happier day when we meet again, I remain, your devoted and loving sister,

Sarah

9

Spring 1858 to Winter 1859

Well supply the sons and daughters
Hymns, no. 244

The three figures blurred in Ann's vision—John, so tall and lean, but filling out in early manhood, smiling the lopsided grin so like his father's; Sarah Jane, nineteen and a little on the thin side, a smattering of freckles on her fair face; Fanny—impetuous, lively Fanny—her dark eyes glittering with excitement and anticipation, her black curls bouncing under a small blue bonnet. Ann looked at them with a strange mixture of pride, amazement, and joy, and a heart swollen with sadness. Once again she stood on a train-station platform bidding goodbye to a loved one—to three dearly loved ones.

The train stood stolidly by, the only reassuring aspect of the long journey ahead of her children, its black immensity and dense clouds of steam declaring its reliability. It wasn't the train that concerned Ann, but the thousands of miles across the ocean, and thence across the better part of the American continent. The thought of her three oldest at the mercies of the sea nearly made her physically ill. Yet at the end of the journey Sarah would be waiting—Sarah and Zion.

"It's to sea I'll be going after all," John grinned down at his mother.

"You always were one to get your way," Ann smiled, trying to keep her voice light, but failing miserably.

The conductor signaled that it was time to board the train. In a moment all seemed confusion, each passenger scrambling to gather up his belongings, hug his relatives, and clamber aboard. Ann clung to each of her children in turn. "John, take care of the girls. Sarah Jane, give your aunt my love and a hug. Fanny, watch your tongue and stay out of trouble."

How can I utter such trivia, Ann thought to herself, *when what I really want to say is I love you, don't get lost, don't get sick, stay close to the Lord, I love you, I LOVE YOU, a thousand other things I'll never be able to say to you again.* But she could only wave now, hold up Elijah while Mary Ann held Emily, and help them wave to the three who crowded around the single grime-clouded window as the train pulled slowly out of the station.

I've sent part of me to Zion, Ann thought, *perhaps the best part.* Reluctantly Ann and her six remaining children turned away from the train which now gathered all its strength and power and with increasing speed soon disappeared down the tracks.

With it disappeared Ann's control. For a moment she hugged Elijah to her and wept openly. The other children gathered forlornly about her, unsure of what to do. Sarah and now three of Ann's children were gone to that distant land—Zion. Did it really exist? To Ann it was still so remote, and while she had harbored glimmers of hope and remembered the promise in the dream, now it seemed so utterly far away, farther than ever before. Now, in addition to supporting the family, Ann had to support the fear of a thousand unknowns as her three eldest gradually moved farther and farther away from her. Now she had no one to rely on except herself. Sarah, John, the girls—one or the other had usually been there to come to her aid, but now Ann was alone in her struggle to keep her family fed and clothed.

Spring wore on, its lively green promise maturing into summer's full bloom, and then the autumn squally season began, making the laundry business difficult to handle. Ann often propped clothes around the kitchen, and the parlor as well, in an effort to dry them. It only made the basement that much more damp and musty. The leaden lump she had carried in her heart since seeing John and the girls off at the station gave no sign of melting. It sometimes yielded when more pressing matters forced themselves upon Ann's consciousness, but until she had news from Zion, the knot of worry persisted.

Finally near the end of the year a letter from Sarah arrived.

Dearest Ann:

Forgive me if this letter seems disjointed and less than grammatical. My heart is filled with a thousand words of anguish and joy, all of which I wish to convey to you, and a mere letter seems so feeble a means to do it.

Sarah Jane and Fanny are here at last in the Valley. Would that they could have arrived together. John made arrangements in New York with an independent wagon train to transport Sarah Jane. Fanny fared less fortunately and came in a handcart company. The captain fancied himself a proper suitor for young Fanny, and when she did not share his notions, it went badly for her. I can only surmise that he thrust every obstacle into her path. To have come by handcart is fearsome enough in itself, but the ordeal that Fanny has endured has come close to taking her young life.

Dear Ann, she is safe now. I shall nurse her as I would my own—indeed, she has always seemed so to me.

I trust John has written to tell you he has elected to stay on in New York. Sarah Jane wept as she told me that he gave her and Fanny the last of his funds so that they could come ahead.

Rejoice, dear sister. Your brood is safe and their long journey ended. My prayers are ever with you, and I'll always remain your loving sister,

Sarah

The letter lightened Ann's heart. She knew her children were safe, and though she ached to help nurse Fanny back to health, she knew she could wish for no more loving care than Sarah would provide. And John—still in New York! She had had no word from him. In spite of a new set of worries, it was a relief and joy to know that Sarah Jane and Fanny were at last in Zion. Ann gathered the children around and, on their knees, they offered up their thanks.

Will watched his children, in imitation of their mother, kneel and bow their heads in prayer. He was not a praying man himself, though Ann had on countless occasions begged him to join them on their knees. Instead he remained stiffly on his feet, his head bowed only slightly. Now a long anticipated worry was a reality—Ann's thoughts had to turn more and more often toward America. How could he combat the ties that now even more securely bound her to that persistent dream?

He turned after their prayer and went into the bedroom. He rummaged for a moment in a far corner of a lower dresser drawer and removed a box. It contained the belt he had refused for so long to wear to bind his hernia in place. Ann had seen the box a hundred times as she opened the drawer, but she was totally unaware of what else was in it. Will opened the box and in a familiar routine sorted, then counted, the coins and pound notes he had accumulated over the years.

In the parlor Ann gave instructions to Lydia. "Be careful on the slick streets, child, and hurry back."

"I'll be that quick, Mum," Lydia assured her.

"Here's the thrupence. I'll tie it into this hankie. Don't undo it before you get to Cranston's."

Lydia nodded, her blue-gray eyes solemn as she moved to the door. "And see that nothing drags about on the ground," Ann called as Lydia's lithe form scampered down the street. Ann closed the door against a persistent wind that howled down the basement steps and hoped Lydia would be able to complete her errand quickly. It was raw outside.

Lydia hugged her thin coat close about her. By the time she reached Cranston's her knuckles ached with the cold. She ducked quickly into the warmth of the small shop, leaned against the door, and breathed on her hands to warm them while a bell above her clanged an announcement of her arrival.

A mostly bald head with wispy fringes of hair above the ears appeared over the counter. Mr. Cranston peered down his nose and through his square spectacles at Lydia. "In a 'urry, are ye, young 'un?"

"It's fearsome cold, sir, and I'll be needin' our clothes for meetin' tomorrow," Lydia announced.

"Tut, tut, but didn't I sell 'em not two hours past." Mr. Cranston grinned as he spoke.

Lydia's heart stopped. Could he truly have sold their Sunday clothes? Whatever would she tell Mum? Lydia fingered the handkerchief with the coins tied inside. A tear started at the corner of each eye.

" 'Ere now, miss, I'm teasin', I am. Yer clothes are in the winder, but they're not sold." Cranston relented. "It's just a bit o' fun I was 'avin'."

The humor was lost on Lydia, but she smiled in relief. Mum would be relieved, too. It was a risk every time Ann brought in their Sunday clothes and pawned them. They had only a week before Mr.

Cranston put them out for sale. Last week they simply hadn't had the thrupence to redeem them, and Lydia had been fearful they would be gone.

The shopowner ambled to the window and gathered up the dresses, caps, wraps, muffs, and hats. Some of the items had seen better days, but they were of sound quality, and though they were all secondhand, they were the Littlefield family's Sunday best, and it was unthinkable that they should lose them.

Lydia unknotted the coins from the limp square of cloth and dropped them on the counter where they spun, then wobbled to rest. Cranston laid the clothes carefully across her waiting arms and tucked up the trailing ties and ribbons.

Lydia bobbed a little curtsy and turned to leave. "I'm beholden, Mr. Cranston," she called out cheerily. "See you next week." She scurried out into the wind.

As she hurried toward home, Lydia buried her face in the armload of clothes, peering up now and then to be sure of her bearings. The wind stung her eyes and made them water. *Maybe Mum'll have a hot cuppa for me when I get home,* Lydia thought. It was probably all there would be to eat. There was rarely any money left, even for food, after they redeemed their clothes.

"We must be spiritually fed, children," Ann constantly reminded them. "Not by bread alone," she was fond of adding.

Lydia's stomach lurched at the thought of bread. Bread would be nice, she mused. A crusty slice would go a long way to quiet her grumbling hunger pangs. Lydia could even smell a warm yeasty aroma as she walked. She looked up to find herself in front of the bakery. She walked another step or two, then stopped in front of the window. She knew she shouldn't stop. Looking only made the hunger worse, but her eyes were drawn to the array of rolls, tarts, muffins, pennywinkles, and golden crusted loaves in the shop window. Lydia leaned her forehead against the glass.

The door to the bakery opened, and a lady stepped out into the street, her figure surrounded momentarily by even more tantalizingly strong, mouth-watering, bakery smells before the wind swept them on down the street. The woman paused, juggling two or three boxes and a large bag. Her eyes lighted suddenly on Lydia.

In a startling moment of clarity the woman read the story in Lydia's wind-stung eyes. She looked down at the small girl, her arms heaped with a collection of clothes, her thin face and threadbare coat practically shouting the child's poverty. Impulsively the lady took the bag of baked goods and laid it quickly atop the clothes in Lydia's arms. Then she moved gracefully into a waiting carriage before Lydia could object—or express thanks. Nearly dizzy with joy, Lydia turned into the wind once again and hurried home with her armload of treasure.

Ann sat at the kitchen table and gazed fondly at the letter. It was not thick, and she knew its contents would be devoured quickly and then the long wait for more news from Zion would begin again. She looked at the return address. It was from Sarah Jane. Would the news be happy? Was Fanny all right? Had they heard from John? Questions darted through Ann's mind, but still she hesitated to open the letter. She wanted to savor every moment of the quiet peace she knew now as she fingered the slim envelope in her trembling hands. This bit of ink and paper had once been in Sarah Jane's hands, had traveled hundreds of miles, crossed a continent, sailed an ocean, and now lay pregnantly before her. She smoothed its white surface, frowned at a smudged fingerprint that sullied its otherwise clean appearance, and then turned it over and gently loosened the seal.

21st October, 1859

Dearest Mother:
  No doubt by the time you receive this letter I shall be married. It is strange how circumstances combine to make us at once both happy and wretched. I delight in knowing that soon I shall be wife to a good man—one William Eddington—and perhaps one day, God willing, a mother in Zion. Yet I grieve to know you will not be here to share in this happy occasion.
  I am consoled to know that you are acquainted with my intended husband. You will recall that he operated the stationer's store during our early days in the South Seas branch. Though somewhat older than myself, he is a good and tender man and is prospering in the confectionery business here in the city. Prior to that he taught many of the Young and Kimball children.
  I know you are anxious for news of Fanny and so will take what space remains to inform you that she is still improving. Aunt Sarah has treated her with what I feel would be your own deep concern. She is not fully recovered yet, but increases in strength by small degrees. Each time I see her we fall about each other's neck and speak about our dear ones yet in England.
  Fanny sends her deepest love, and I join her in that heartfelt message. Your loving daughter,

Sarah Jane

74

Ann smiled, sighed, and reread the letter. At various times throughout the day she took it out of her apron and read it again. The Lord was good to her, she concluded. Her lot was not easy, but then again, whose was? She had a testimony of the true religion and nine healthy children, and not a one of them a plague to her as some were to their parents. And now a daughter was to marry—in the Church—to a man she cared for and who could—and would—provide for her. Truly, in things that made life richest, Ann felt herself wealthy indeed.

Even Will was a blessing in some ways. He kept her ever pointed in the right direction—she could turn neither to the right nor to the left in defending the Church. By constantly throwing obstacles in her path, he had fortified her, pushed her constantly into seeking the Lord's help, forced her to build an unshakable faith. Poor Will—he'd only made stronger what he had hoped to weaken.

On his return home from work that evening, she looked at him carefully. She was shocked to suddenly realize that they had been married thirteen years. Even allowing for the difference in their ages, Will seemed to have grown old beyond his time. His hair was nearly entirely gray, and the lines about his mouth had been etched deeply by the terrible bouts of pain he suffered more and more frequently. Ann fixed his supper and served it to him. When he'd eaten, she laid a hand gently upon his shoulder.

"How did it go today, Will? You look that beazled."

Will closed his eyes, leaned back against the chair, and nodded. "The days grow no shorter, that's a surety."

"I've a bit of ironing to finish up, but then I'll heat a brick and wrap it for you. Go along with you now and read for a while." She patted his shoulder. "Then I'll see to it."

"I've not the strength nor the inclination to object," Will replied. He pushed back his chair and stood slowly, pressing one hand against his lower abdomen.

Ann watched him move carefully out of the room. She frowned. How he tolerated so much pain she couldn't understand. He really should use that belt he kept in the drawer, or see a doctor. Perhaps there was some medication he could take or a better kind of belt. It had been years since he'd been to a doctor, and possibly a different one could help. But she felt sure Will would do neither. What was it that kept a man clinging to his own appraisal of things? Will, once he'd made up his mind, adhered to his ideas as though they were a second skin. To change them or make room for new ones would be as painful for him as major surgery without an anesthetic.

Thank goodness, Ann mused as she lay the ironing board across the backs of two chairs, we've had little illness in this house. Other than John's long bout with typhoid, and an occasional case of sniffles or slight fever, the children had been remarkably healthy. Ann added that blessing to her mental list and expressed her gratitude in her silent, brief, but frequent conversations with the Lord during the day and in her whispered, kneeling prayers at night. And then, as if the devil's own angels had been listening, David fell seriously ill that next week.

Mary Ann summoned Ann early one morning to see David, who lay, moaning softly, on his cot. "He feels hot, Mum. Shall I wet a cloth?"

"Do that, dear, and I'll check him over."

David's face was flushed, yet he was white around the mouth. Ann pulled up his nightshirt and inspected his body for a rash. There was none that she could see, nor anything that appeared to be out of the ordinary. She covered her son and pressed her hand to his forehead. It was very warm. Little tremors of worry began to move in the pit of Ann's stomach.

David could tell her nothing beyond the fact that he "hurt all over, and my head the worst of all." Ann tried to get him to sip some chamomile tea, but it hurt his head too much to raise it from the pillow. Ann spooned the tea into his mouth a bit at a time, but he took only a few swallows before he complained that it hurt to swallow, too.

Ann set Mary Ann and Lydia to tend the twins, but sent Joseph off to school as usual. She spent much of the day checking on David. There seemed to be little change until that night, when Will went in to see him.

"Ann, come quickly! Look—look at his back," Will demanded, the worry evident in his voice.

Ann looked and her hand flew involuntarily to her mouth. David's back was arched up off the bed, and his neck and head strained in an unnatural bend as well. David either could not hear them now or could not answer their pleas to speak to them.

"I'm fetching the doctor," Will turned abruptly. "I've never seen the likes of this before."

"Wait, Will," Ann called after him. "How will we pay him? I've no money in the house."

"Hang the money! That boy is sick, as bad off as he can be. He's got to have help now."

"Let me call the elders to bless him," Ann pleaded.

"Are you daft, woman? Your son is at death's door and you want to fool around with that gibberish?"

"Will, please! I know what I'm doing," Ann insisted.

"We've no time for this. I'm fetching the doctor." He threw his scarf around his neck, slid his cap over his head, grabbed his coat, and rushed out the door, thrusting his arms into his coat sleeves as he strode quickly down the street.

Ann agonized over the situation. Will would most certainly berate her for summoning the elders should she decide to do so. It might even be embarrassing to him should he return with the doctor and find the elders in the midst of their administration. And though Will would probably become quite ugly over the whole thing, Ann trusted instinctively in the priesthood administration she knew the elders were authorized to perform. She drew a deep breath and made her decision.

"Lydia, come here quickly." Ann wrapped a shawl around her daughter's shoulders, then covered that with a cape. She spoke hurriedly as she tied a bonnet to Lydia's head. "Run as fast as you can to the elders' flat. Fetch them here at once. Tell them to bring their oil—that it's for David Littlefield."

Lydia scurried off into the night.

An hour later Will returned. The doctor had promised to come as soon as he could. In anguish he explained to Ann.

"Will, it's all right. Don't upset yourself so."

"But, David," Will insisted. "How long can he suffer with his back contorted so—"

Ann led him gently to the bedroom. They paused at the doorway, and Will's misery gradually gave way to amazement as he took in the scene. Propped up in his bed, David sat comfortably sipping a steaming cup of chamomile.

10

February 1860 to Christmas 1861

Streams, ever copious, are gliding along
Hymns, no. 182

"Lydia, don't tease so. Give it to me," Ann pleaded.

Lydia's eyes danced with mischief as she darted from one end of the table to the other, staying just out of reach of her mother's hands. "You missed me, you missed me, now you have to kiss me," she giggled and chanted.

Laughing and breathless, Ann feinted to one side, then quickly ducked under the table and grabbed at Lydia's skirt. "I've got you, scalawag," Ann announced triumphantly. "Now let's have the letter."

"My kiss first," Lydia demanded.

"Here's your kiss"—Ann pecked her daughter on the cheek—"and a squeeze to go with it. Now off with you while I read what news from Sarah Jane."

Lydia reluctantly but happily gave up her game, handed the envelope to her mother, and scampered off to find another playmate.

Ann plopped into a chair by the table and fanned herself for a moment with the envelope. As she did so she caught a glimpse of the return address. The letter was not from Sarah Jane—it was from John! With none of her usual savoring restraint, Ann ripped open the envelope, reading the single sheet of closely written lines quickly.

Dearest Mother:

At long last I take pen in hand to tell you I will soon be in a position to continue my interrupted journey to Zion.

On the chance you may not know, I must tell you I had to send Sarah Jane and Fanny on ahead soon after our arrival in New York last year. I had not the money to continue with them, and gave them every farthing I had to ensure their proper escort and sustenance for the journey. I resolved to stay here and obtain suitable employment in order to earn the necessary funds to continue on to the Valley.

It has been difficult to get and keep work here in New York. If it isn't my limey accent, it's my religion that impedes my progress. But I have applied myself with all diligence, making the most of every opportunity, and do promise you that I will once again be on my way with the arrival of spring.

I implore your forgiveness for failing to write before this. I could not bring myself to disappoint you. Nor did I want to spend even the few pence—or, as the Americans put it, pennies—to send a letter before I could be more definite about my situation.

I think of you often, and of Sarah Jane and Fanny as well. I can only pray they have arrived in the Valley safely and that all is well with them. God willing, they have been more attentive in letter writing than have I.

Though I long to know how it fares with you, Mother, I do not advise that you write until you hear from me once again—this time from Salt Lake City. If you are able, I beg you to let Sarah Jane and Fanny know of my impending arrival.

Until in God's time we may meet and embrace once more, I remain,

Your dutiful and obedient son,

John

Ann clasped the letter to her breast and wiped at her eyes and nose. The long months of not knowing, of worrying, of imagined catastrophes and ill fortune melted away in the brief few moments it took to read John's letter.

A peaceful swelling of contentment filled Ann's heart as she contemplated the answer to yet another of her prayers. As she looked back over the years since her baptism, she could not say her life was any easier because of the gospel—only that there was an inner joy, a steady confidence, a growing contentment that seemed to increase with each passing year.

The unending physical labor to support her family, the constant defense of her religion against the persistent pressure that Will applied to thwart her devotion to the Church, had proved only to be the refiner's fire, not the consuming discouragement and defeat he had hoped for. Where once Ann had come nearly to the point of hatred for the obstacles her husband seemed to almost daily pile in front of her, now she felt instead the sweet, calming influence of the gospel; where once she might have become embittered and rebellious, she had now become peaceful and trusting. She even felt a certain pity for Will's stubborn contempt for what she knew was the truth. And as much as Ann longed to join her children in Zion, she was content for the time knowing that they were there among the Saints. The promise that she, too, would one day dwell in Zion still seemed very far from reality. Will became daily more hostile to the Church, and Ann still labored to feed the family. Yet a quiet assurance ran through her veins. She had gone to the Lord too often in seemingly hopeless situations to doubt him now. When the time was right, the Lord would provide.

In the meantime, the months slid by. Some days seemed endlessly long—from dark to dark Ann worked, tended the children, encouraged David and Joseph in their studies, soothed an aching Will when he returned from work, and dropped to her knees in prayer each night. And yet some days brought their own special joys—a letter from Zion; a visit from Mary Ann (now, as her sisters had done before her, working to add a few pence to the family's income); a quiet happiness as Ann sat amid her children in Sunday meetings as the elders preached and exhorted and rejoiced while they shared the knowledge of the restored gospel.

And there were always special occasions like birthdays to look forward to, such as Lydia's tenth coming up soon. Ann wanted it to be special, for soon Lydia would follow Mary Ann to become a maid. Sweet Lydia—so young to be sent off to work—but a friend of Mary Ann's employer needed a live-in housemaid, and Mary Ann suggested Lydia. Her proposed employer would be away on the Continent for a month or two, but when she returned, it was agreed that Lydia would become an addition to their household staff.

Lydia's birthday dawned, a cloudy day, but inside the basement flat Ann spread as much sunshine as she could. She'd hoarded a penny here and a penny there and purchased a bit of white fabric for a pinafore to cover Lydia's linsey-woolsey frock. There was not sugar enough to make a sweet treat, but Ann had been able to put aside enough flour to make some biscuits to accompany their celebration supper of potato soup and hot tea.

When Ann placed the gift, done up in brown butcher-paper and string, in Lydia's lap, the child's eyes widened in surprise. She clapped her hands, then ran them cautiously over the package.

"Come on, Lyd! You've got to open it somewhen!"

The other children echoed David's sentiments.

Four-year-old Elijah rushed around the table to Lydia's chair. "I'll help you, Lyd."

"I can do it, Lije!" She began gently pulling at the string and undoing the wrapper. "Soor! A new pinney!" Lydia exclaimed.

"Let me see, let me see," Emily chanted.

Lydia obligingly held up the new garment. Once again Elijah reached for it.

"Careful, Lije. You'll grub it up with those mucky hands."

"That's none of a problem. Mum can wash it in her nexdy's bucking," Joseph said.

They all laughed merrily and scrambled from the table to play in the parlor. While Ann cleaned up the supper table, the children enjoyed the evening's celebration. Will looked up from his paper now and then to watch as they played a sort of hide-and-seek game accompanied by a song:

> Hussing and bussing will not do,
> But go to the gate, knock and ring—
> Please, Mrs. Brown, is Nellie within?

Within a few days of the birthday celebration, Lydia tearfully took leave of her family. She was somewhat excited yet fearful about the change. But Ann assured her it would be a comfort to sleep alone in her own bed in a warm house, eat in a kitchen with a well-stocked larder, and never lack for anything. Lydia nodded solemnly, not believing it for a moment.

In Lydia's first few days away from home, homesickness engulfed her like great ocean waves. There seemed always to be a lump of lead in her stomach, and she ate hardly any of the array of food that the servants downed noisily after the master and mistress had been served. What terrified her most was bedding down at night among strangers, and she missed little Emily's warm body snuggled next to hers during the night.

But gradually she became accustomed to her lot, and the knot in her stomach loosened. Before she knew it, Christmas had crept up on them. The housekeeper had promised Lydia she could go home on Christmas Eve and spend all of Christmas day with her family. Lydia flew through her chores on Christmas Eve day, humming carols and flitting from room to room in preparation for her employer's expected Christmas company. She dropped to her knees to polish table legs, then stood on tiptoe to flick at mites of dust atop the picture frames. Late in the afternoon the housekeeper called Lydia to her.

Breathless, Lydia planted herself in front of Mrs. Leeds.

"You've done well in our employ, ducky. 'Ere's your wage." She counted a few coins into Lydia's palm. "Now come with me. I've a bit of something for your Christmas."

Surprised, Lydia followed Mrs. Leeds out the back door. The housekeeper stopped in front of the coal bin.

"There, Lydia. You may have a lump of coal—whichever you choose. But mind, you've a long ways to walk."

Nevertheless Lydia did not hesitate. She stooped and, with some difficulty, picked up the largest lump of coal she could see. With heavily laden arms but a light heart, Lydia set off toward home.

At the Littlefields' Mary Ann had arrived to joyous shouts and welcome hugs. Ann asked if Mary Ann had seen her sister on her way, anxious for them all to be home together. The younger children gathered around Mary Ann while she described in detail the preparations she had been a part of in her employer's home. The children loved to hear these stories and always listened with mouths agape and eyes wide with wonder as she related the anecdotes and stories of her life away from home.

"Will there be snapdragons?" Joseph questioned.

"Of course! There's scarce a home without snapdragons this night!"

"Tell us, tell us," Elijah and Emily chimed.

Mary Ann laughed and gathered them closer to her. "Well, first you take a great silver platter. Then you scatter on top of it lots of plump, juicy raisins—like these." To their delight she plopped a raisin into each of their hands, which was quickly transferred to their mouths. "Then the master pours over the brandy and lights it with a long match. The raisins glow with a blue flame, tinged with orange and yellow. Soor, it's a sight for the eyes!"

"Then what, Mary?" Emily gurgled.

"Why then, little nipper, the master carries around the platter, and everyone tries to snatch a raisin without getting burned!"

They all sighed with the elegance of it all.

The parlor door opened and a blast of cold, sea-sharpened winter air entered along with Will.

"Father! Merry Christmas, Father," the twins sang out. "Come listen to our Mary Ann."

"Hold on. I've an errand first." Will strode into the kitchen, followed by his brood. In the middle of the table he placed a bundle, then unwrapped it to reveal a fat chicken.

"Will!" Ann exclaimed. "Chicken—I had hoped for a rabbit perhaps, but chicken!"

The children too, squealed with delight. Ann smiled, relieved to have a small truce once again. She patted his hand and thanked him. "It will be a special Christmas now, Will. We've food for a near banquet and our children are home—or will be when Lydia gets here. What could be keeping the child?"

The large lump of coal was keeping Lydia. She struggled and staggered with her heavy burden, and could walk only a short way before laying it down to rest. Her arms and back ached with the effort. But she was determined to wrestle it home. It would keep them all warm for the better part of the day, and that was a gift Lydia just could not relinquish.

She was not yet out of the finer section of the city. Every so often she passed carriages waiting out in front of the fine homes, the horses standing with tinges of frost in their manes and jets of steam rhythmically puffing out their nostrils, the driver snuggled down in muffler and scarf.

Gradually Lydia worked her way closer to her neighborhood. It was getting dark. She had tried holding the coal so as to keep her coat and frock clean, but now it was all she could do to carry the leaden lump. Once again she stopped to rest, placing the coal carefully at her feet. She rubbed her arms and shook them to throw off the ache. To her right she noticed a beggar hunkered down in the doorway of a closed shop. His threadbare rags could not possibly keep him warm. He could not see her, as he was blind, but his head moved in short jerks from side to side, sensing that someone was near.

Lydia's heart swelled with pity and understanding. In a few moments she would be home with her family, and they would burn the coal. The poor blind man would most likely spend the night in the doorway, cold and alone. Lydia fingered the coins in her pocket. Her mother needed the money, too, Lydia knew only too well. But it was Christmas! She had been given a gift; now it was her turn. Timidly she approached the old man. She bent, and dropped a farthing into the cup.

The sound of the coin ringing in the otherwise empty tin startled the man, and he croaked a hearty "Thank ye, God bless."

Now Lydia hoisted the coal into her arms once again. She was sure it was her imagination, but the lump suddenly seemed much lighter, and she walked quickly now in the gathering darkness toward home.

At last Lydia arrived at the flat's basement steps. Gingerly she picked her way down the dark stairs, feeling rather than seeing her way. On the next to the last step she stumbled, falling heavily against the door. The noise brought Ann, Will, and all the children to the door as Ann flung it wide. Lydia stood framed in the pale light, smudged and blackened from head to toe.

"What on earth, child!"

"It's coal I've brung ye, Mum! It was my Christmas gift from Mrs. Leeds, and I brung the biggest of the lot!"

Emily peered out from behind her mother's skirts. "You got coal for Christmas, Lyd?"

11

Early 1862 to December 1863

Every human tie may perish

Hymns, no. 212

Early in the New Year another noise at the door caused Joseph to look up from his book. No one else seemed to have heard anything, though, so he returned to his reading. Then it came again. It was a knock, feeble, but nevertheless quite real. He hurried to open the door. There was something familiar about the figure who stood there, but Joseph could not remember ever seeing him before.

"Fetch your mother," the man croaked as Joseph studied him.

"Mum," he hollered, "there's a man what's come to see you."

Ann hurried to the door. She stared for a moment in bewilderment, then blurted, "Merciful heavens—William!" She grabbed her brother's arm and pulled him into the parlor.

Will had by this time reached the door also. They led William in and sat him down on the horsehair sofa. He smiled weakly at them and then bent over in a paroxysm of coughing. When he could speak he explained.

"Forgive me, Ann. I'd not intrude if I had naun else to do."

"William, hush. How could we count my own brother an intrusion?"

"I've been turned out of my room, Ann. Got behind in the rent, and the landlady isn't fond of nonpaying guests."

"Where are your things? Have you a valise outside?" Will asked.

William shook his head wearily. "The landlady took what few things I had left to sell against what I owed her."

Will and Ann exchanged glances. Before Ann could speak, Will drew Ann aside. "You'll still not get any of my wages if we take him in, Ann. But if you want to put him up for a while, I'll not object."

Ann nodded. She was grateful for even that much. At least she would not have to turn her brother away, even though it might add to her problems. She knelt down in front of William. "You must stay here, William. You've a home with us for as long as you need until you're back on your feet again."

William's eyes misted as he whispered hoarsely, "Bless you both."

The children stared at their uncle. It had been years since William had visited, and only David had any recollection of him. Ann introduced the twins and Joseph, all three born since William had last seen Ann's family.

They talked for a while, exchanging what news Ann had of Sarah and James and his wife in America, telling William of the Fry children's emigration to Zion. Will watched Ann carefully as he always did when she spoke of her three eldest children. Though she spoke calmly enough, there was a certain tensing of her body, a glint in her eye, a lifting of the chin that conveyed her deep interest in America more eloquently than any words she uttered. The woman had never given up.

Will closed his eyes and snorted in irritation. There would be no easing Ann's devotion to either her children or the Church. She would never voluntarily leave it, he knew that now. The years of forcing her to hard labor to feed their family, the demands, the threats, the embarrassment—none of these had produced the effects Will knew must come about if he were to force her obedience.

With a stubbornness nearly equal to his wife's, Will clung to a vision of returning to the nearly idyllic marriage they had enjoyed before the Church had ruined it all. He rarely thought of anything else except finding a way to eliminate that irritating influence from their lives.

If only the plaguing hernia would leave him a moment's peace he might be able to think more clearly to find the answer. If only Ann could be diverted from her fanaticism and apply all that zeal to some cause other than that all-demanding religion. Then, with Will directing their lives, the boys could really make something of themselves instead of throwing themselves away on a church that could only bring them unhappiness.

Even William's stay with them would not have to interfere. William probably only needed a rest and some steady care and he would be back on his own. But Will worried about his own ill health. He struggled daily to keep going. The pain never seemed far from him. It lurked just beneath the surface, always ready to fasten him in its unrelenting grip, and when it did its worst, it squeezed the strength and energy out of him, leaving him drained and exhausted. Ann was constantly tending to both Will and William in their bad moments, and it kept her busier than ever.

But William's presence in the house in some ways eased Ann's burden. William was anxious to help where he could, and did whatever his failing strength allowed. But he also brought additional problems. Now the few coins Lydia's employment brought in were only enough to cover the extra food to feed another mouth. William ate little, but Ann felt duty-bound to feed him as well as she possibly could and try to improve his frail health. As she had done for John, she put up a cot in the kitchen. He had little or no privacy, but William seemed content with his little corner in the Littlefield household.

In addition to providing bed and board for William, the Littlefields readily opened their doors to the ever-changing pairs of elders who directed the affairs of the Portsea Branch. The Mormons seemed to have no end to those who came to direct the small branch, proselyte new members, and promote their gathering to Zion. As fast as they wore out one bunch, they sent another to replace it. Zion must contain a constantly shifting population, Will concluded.

The latest arrival had included a new president for the branch, a rather young man named David Kimball. Though he was young, his hair was already thinning. His large head sat squarely on wide shoulders and a stockily built body. He wore the muttonchop whiskers and long, dark coat with lightly colored trousers that were favored in the current fashion. He had bedded down with them the first night or two until he had located his own quarters. Then he began to visit fairly often. He seemed rather fond of Ann, calling her "mother."

Will tolerated the visits. He knew they always raised Ann's hopes that he would turn the discussion to the gospel, and it amused him to dance around the topic without getting specific. Besides, he relished the direct news from the States, getting tidbits of information that often did not appear in his paper until days later. Right now he had a passing interest in the war that was raging in the States. On one of Elder Kimball's first visits he had questioned him.

"Any war news, Mr. Kimball?"

"A bit, Mr. Littlefield. McLellan seems to have bungled things again, and Lincoln has replaced him. It was quite the popular topic of conversation in New York as I came through."

"Mr. Lincoln does seem to have his troubles with his generals, doesn't he? The Confederates, on the other hand, seem to be getting along rather well under Lee, if Vicksburg is any indication."

"I'm grateful John got away from New York before the hostilities erupted," Ann interjected.

"That's right, mother!" Kimball turned to remark. "I'd forgotten you have children in America! But there's no need to worry. No Confederates have gotten as far north as New York."

"Just the same, I'm glad John's well away from it."

"I suppose no mother ever enjoys sending a son to war," Elder Kimball acknowledged.

Will asked a few more questions which Elder Kimball was pleased to answer. Then he excused himself, shook hands with Will, planted a kiss on Ann's forehead, and took leave of them.

"A pleasant chap," Will acknowledged after his departure.

"He certainly takes no time in getting acquainted," Ann commented. "He's barely arrived in the branch and is already well-known to nearly every member."

"I suppose he's a Zionist, too," Will offered. "Don't any of your Mormon ministers advocate staying put?"

"Elders, Will, not ministers," Ann reminded him.

"Whatever," Will replied. "You don't still harbor hopes of joining your children in America?"

Ann looked closely at Will. She had no desire to lie to him, yet she knew an affirmative answer would only anger him. Their latest truce had stretched to a long unbroken period of years, and Ann had no desire to disturb the peace of it.

"I miss them very much, Will," Ann parried.

"That's not quite what I asked, Ann," Will persisted. "But never you mind. You know well enough America is out of the question."

Ann nodded. She knew it, yet somehow she could not submerge her longing to join her children. But she wanted more than anything else to avoid an argument, so she let the matter drop. She buried herself once again in the all-consuming daily struggle to provide for her family and nurse William and now, ever increasingly, Will, when he suffered his hernia attacks.

As time slipped by Ann took more and more enjoyment from the intermittent letters from the Valley. They sustained her as nothing else did. But one day a letter arrived that threatened to destroy all the peace of mind Ann had so carefully nurtured through the years:

My dear Ann:

With what heaviness of heart and deep anguish I take my pen in hand at this time, I cannot begin to describe. Would God that there were some easier way to convey this message to you.

My wife, your daughter Sarah Jane, has died in childbirth. We obtained the services of the best doctor in the Valley but all was to no avail. The baby, a boy who lives, was turned wrong, and in the difficult birthing, we lost her.

What scarce comfort I may offer, I do so with all my heart. Sarah Jane spoke of you often. She requested near the end that I tell you it was all right—her passing.

I will endeavor to raise up the boy as I feel Sarah would have done. I remain, in mutual grief and sincerity, your son-in-law,

William Eddington

Involuntarily Ann cried out. She felt as though her heart had been wrenched from her breast, and the pain sent nauseating waves reeling through her body. At first the shock was so great she could hardly breathe, and when the children came running to ask about her cry she found it difficult to put the tragedy into words. When at last she told them, as briefly as possible, they looked uncomprehendingly at her.

William, too, was shocked by her reaction, and had no words to comfort her. He sat numbly on his cot as Ann sobbed great racking sobs, her hands clenching the sad letter.

It was thus that Will found her on his return from work.

"Ann, Ann, what is it?" he asked.

Ann could only hand Will the letter. As he read it, he tried to feel what Ann might be feeling, but long years of hardening his heart to her needs made it difficult. He sat heavily in a chair near her. Awkward in the face of her grief he could only mutter, "Ann, don't cry. It will all come round."

But Ann was numb to everything but the exquisite blade of pain that cut relentlessly around and around her heart, never seeming to complete its efforts to separate completely her heart from her body, always cutting through new nerve endings and tender flesh. At length she realized the pain was there to stay.

She arose and poured a small amount of water in her washbasin. Slowly she dipped her hands into the water and then ran her hands over her face. Repeatedly she splashed the water over her ravaged eyes, the coolness of the liquid barely registering in her grief-filled mind.

Mechanically she returned to routine chores, and somehow the day ended—then another, and another. As though her mind was detached from her body, she laundered and cooked, cleaned and marketed. Ann withdrew behind a wall of grief that repulsed the combined efforts of everyone in the family. Will realized only time would ultimately heal Ann's pain, but nevertheless he felt impelled to attempt a shock treatment. It went a long way toward accomplishing his purpose.

Without any preliminary warning or announcements, Will very quietly one payday laid his wages on the table. Ann stared at the coins. Bewildered at first, she wondered where they had come from, then realized with a faint surge of shock what had happened. Will, after all these years, had once again taken on full support of his family.

A great flood of mixed emotions ran through Ann. She was relieved to feel something other than the ache that still gripped her from Sarah Jane's death. A wild desire to laugh and a sudden exhilaration at release from the bondage of grief (as well as that of her long battle to sustain her family) warred for the upper hand within Ann's mind. She rejoiced in Will's capitulation, and even felt a certain surge of gratitude. But at the same time she recognized an uncharacteristic surge of resentment. How easily he had laid those coins down—how arbitrarily he had suddenly resumed a responsibility that should have been his all along. At his whim he had withdrawn his wages; at his whim he had restored them. For a brief instant Ann considered flinging the coins at him, refusing his help and continuing the struggle alone. She wanted to cry at him, "Now—now, after the many times I could have dropped down and died of fatigue, when I had to bite my fist to keep from sobbing when the children went to bed hungry and moaned in their sleep because of it, now you simply lay your wages down, without a word?"

But the impulse faded, and just as quietly as Will had laid them down, Ann took them up, pocketed them, and used them. Neither one mentioned the incident to the other.

12

Early 1864 to May 1864

For God remembers still his promise
made of old

Hymns, no. 62

Ann wrestled with her emotions. Will's sudden capitulation regarding his wages eased her workload considerably. She still did some laundry, for even with Will's wages they could use the money. With four children still under their roof there was always a need for something. But the work was different now—there was less urgency about it, and Ann could work less feverishly. But she still grieved over Sarah Jane's death. The worst of that was over, too, yet sometimes the pain still returned to steal her breath and fill her eyes with tears. And she still worried over William. She could afford to feed him a little better now, but it was not having the hoped-for beneficial effect. A pall had fallen over her normally determined spirits. Even attendance at Church meetings, normally refreshing, couldn't seem to ease the gloom of Ann's days.

At a fast and testimony meeting one evening, Ann was especially dejected. The Portsea Branch was once again preparing to send as many of its members as possible to Zion, and a certain air of excitement, of expectancy, was beginning to build. Ann was not immune to the excitement, and for years had been able to rejoice with her fellow Saints, to exult in their anticipation and joyous expectations. But this year that was nearly impossible.

"My God," she prayed silently, "what am I to do? How can I live through another exodus from this dear branch without our being with them? How can I survive the knowledge that they will be leaving for Zion, and that I must cut myself off from them all?"

Ann longed to bear her own testimony. Zion was on everyone's lips, every testimony was filled with fervent commitments to make every effort to join the Saints in America. But Ann was no nearer to that goal now than she had been years ago. How could she bear her testimony when she could make no such commitment, when she could not declare her intentions of joining them, this year or any year? Instead she stood and requested a favorite hymn:

> O Zion, when I think of thee
> I long for pinions like the dove,
> And mourn to think that I should be
> so distant from the land I love.

The tears welled in Ann's eyes as she listened to the Saints sing. Her throat was too tight with choked emotion to sing herself. Though she struggled to contain them, tears slid down her cheeks. Emily snuggled next to her mother and in solemn sympathy reached up and wiped the tears from her face.

After the meeting David Kimball walked home with them. Unspoken but heavy in the air was Ann's longing to be with the Saints, to follow the Prophet's counsel, to see John and Fanny and the grandson for whom Sarah Jane had sacrificed her life. David seemed to sense her silent prayers, and shortly before they arrived at the flat, he stopped and turned to Ann. Puzzled at his hesitation, she looked at him with eyebrows raised. He looked down into her eyes and said, "Mother, you are to go to Zion this year."

Ann blinked and searched David Kimball's face. He smiled back at her unflinchingly. She had heard correctly. An elder of the Church, a duly ordained and authorized messenger of the restored gospel, had told her the time had come! In the year of our Lord 1864, the Littlefields were to go to Zion!

David, behind his smiling countenance, was wondering how he had come to make such a promise. He knew of Will's scarcely concealed hostility, knew Will Littlefield would sooner go to his grave than humble himself to join the Mormons. But he also knew better than to question a prompting that had come from the Spirit. He swallowed and made arrangements with Ann to discuss all possible avenues at a later date.

Ann's mind reeled under this new onslaught. How much more could she handle? Sarah Jane's death, William's illness, Will's hostility to the Church, and her own despair at being denied the sanctuary of Zion—now David Kimball, apparently in response to spiritual promptings, had told her they were to go to Zion! Ann counted backward. In sudden elation she realized it had been ten years since the dream wherein she had been promised Zion. The promise had been there all these years, a steady source of comfort and reassurance, though she had begun to feel the time frame was somehow wrong. She knew Will would have to be converted before the promise could be fulfilled, and she knew at that moment that he was as far from that as he had ever been, perhaps farther.

Yet there it was. David had received the same prompting, and seemingly on the same schedule the Lord had revealed to Ann years earlier. She had never spoken of the dream to anyone. She had hugged it to herself in absolute secrecy, afraid that translation into words would shatter the promise and bring it to naught. Somehow Ann would have to find the faith to trust that the Lord knew what he was doing. "Will is his child, too. The Lord will bring him to an understanding," she concluded to herself.

At their meeting David approached the situation carefully.

"Have you any means at all to pay your passage?"

Ann shook her head. "Nothing. Not a farthing. But even the money does not worry me so much as Will. Do you have any idea, David, how it may come about that Will might yield himself up to the Lord's direction?"

David looked at her blankly. "Will? I've never supposed that he would do any such thing."

Ann stared in return. "But I've never considered any other possibility. I cannot go to Zion without my husband!"

"Have you any reason to believe Will is close to a change of heart?"

"No. In fact, he has never seemed further from it. But surely if the Lord has promised this, has prompted you to reveal it to me, surely he will do something about Will."

"I feel strongly, mother, that it is you—and your children—who are given the promise. You must make up your mind to that."

"Leave my husband? Surely you can't be suggesting such a thing!"

"What have you done to teach him the gospel?" David asked her.

Ann gathered her startled wits about her and thought. "I've taught him what I could, talked about our meetings. The children and I talked doctrine in his hearing. I've brought pamphlets, tracts, even the *Millennial Star* home. I've left the Book of Mormon about, encouraging him to read it, even hoping he'd pick it up by mistake and get interested."

"And how did Will respond?"

"At first he ignored all our efforts. Then he became irritated, and finally genuinely angry. He threw out whatever material from the Church he found."

"And did you give up at these displays of anger?"

"No—never! I've prayed nearly constantly for him. I've scarce talked with the Lord these long years without pleading for my husband. Surely the Lord has heard those pleas!"

"We both know he has. But you know also that the Lord will force no man to heaven. Ann, don't you see? You've done all that is humanly possible. The Lord asks no more of you. He wills that you go to Zion. Isn't that what you truly want?"

"More than anything!" Ann agreed. "But alone?"

"You'll hardly be alone. Every ship carries hundreds of fellow Saints. No woman is alone when she is under the protection of the priesthood."

Ann shook her head. It was unheard of for a woman to leave her husband. How could the Lord require such an action from her? "Please, David, I must think about this—and pray."

He nodded. "Search the scriptures, mother. And when you do, be mindful of Matthew, the tenth chapter, verses thirty-four to thirty-eight."

Ann looked up the scriptures he had mentioned as soon as she had readied herself for bed. They contained much food for thought. "A man's foes shall be they of his own household," one of the verses read. And a woman's too?

Ann lay awake long into the night. She had whispered her prayers quietly, but with all the hunger of a soul in despair. There seemed to be no immediate response, and she climbed wearily into bed to stare into the darkness and sort out her feelings. She thought back to the dream. Had it been from the Lord? She'd never doubted it at the time, nor since, didn't really doubt it now, especially after David Kimball had received an identical impression. Then if it was from the Lord, what about Will? Ann had tried every means at her disposal to love her husband into the Church. She'd walked that terribly precarious line of divided loyalty, trying on one hand to be a dutiful wife, an obedient wife, yet unable to deny her conviction of the truth of the gospel and the restored Church. Now the Lord seemed to be telling her she had done what she could and to leave Will to him. What did the Lord have in mind? What did he know that she didn't? She smiled in the dark at that thought. And if she could bring herself to leave Will, how would she find the money needed for passage? She could not very well ask Will to finance her desertion. Desertion! The word turned her cold. Yet gradually the weight of the Lord's promise to her left her no other decision. To ignore his will for her was unthinkable, too. A familiar warmth and certainty filled her veins and chased away the cold. Ann's prayers had too often been answered for her to doubt the Lord or his mysterious ways. She turned on her side and, the finality of her decision pressing in upon her, cried softly until sleep overtook her.

As soon as possible she arranged another meeting with David Kimball.

"I know now it's right to go. But even when I know it's right, it hasn't made things easier," Ann confided to David.

He looked at her red-rimmed and swollen eyes. "The way is never easy, mother. I don't know why the Lord requires so much of some, and seemingly so little of others."

"Does it have to be *now?*"

"Faith. Isn't that always the ultimate answer? Do you think it will be any easier at any other time?"

"But what about the money? And more important, what about William, my brother? How can I leave him right now?"

"The Lord asks nothing of us that we cannot accomplish," David reiterated. "We must move forward with our plans and place our faith in him. Try to think of the end rather than the means. See yourself in Zion. See yourself and your children all together once again."

"That seems to be the only bright prospect in this whole business," Ann sighed.

"We must consider every possible means of obtaining the necessary funds. Have you any relatives who have gone on to America before you?"

"A sister, Sarah; my brother James and his family—they all seem to be struggling to keep body and soul together. My son John is there, and a daughter, Fanny—Fanny has not been well since she arrived, and my sister Sarah cares for her. I'm sure they have naun to spare. You know my eldest daughter Sarah Jane died last year in childbirth."

"Yes, I recall." He paused for a moment in silent sympathy. "To whom was Sarah Jane married? What circumstances is he in?"

"She married William Eddington, a convert from this conference—"

"Eddington!" David interrupted her. "I know him well. He taught some of my brothers and sisters. He has gone into business for himself now. Perhaps he could help!"

"Ask my daughter's husband? I don't feel right—"

"Mother, he may be the answer. Many of the Saints in better circumstances are only too happy to help wherever they can. And certainly we must contact your son John."

"When he last wrote he was working in a store in Salt Lake City—Walker Brothers, I believe he said. But he's planning to marry in the fall—he's been putting a bit aside for that."

"We can only give him the opportunity, mother. We must not decide for him."

Ann agreed that David should write to John, and to William Eddington. He promised to post the letters immediately.

In the meantime, Ann lived with the daily fear that Will would discover her plans. She felt keenly a sense of betrayal of her husband. She had struggled with the decision—knew it was right and what the Lord expected of her, yet still felt a nagging guilt that refused to yield to reason. Adding to that guilt was the obvious pain of Will's long-neglected hernia.

There was no let-up now. Will had no other choice but to wear the despised belt—the discomfort of wearing it paled in comparison to the pain he fought against every day. The belt would keep him going now, he was convinced.

Ann read the pain in his eyes. She noted, too, as he undressed for bed, that he wore the belt, and realized how he must be suffering to give in to its constraints. He repeatedly repulsed her efforts to have him consider medical attention.

William, too, appeared to be failing. In spite of the tender care and attentive nursing, he seemed to spend more and more time on his cot. Any effort at all brought on terrible paroxysms of coughing that left him gasping and exhausted. Ann cursed the dampness of the basement flat and tried to keep a fire going constantly in the grate to dry and warm the air. But it became apparent that William would never recover fully from his affliction.

Ann's worry over Will and William tossed her back and forth. They both seemed to need her more and more, yet she was in the midst of plans to leave them both. At times she felt she might lose her mind. To add to the confusion, David Kimball received a response to his pleas for funds for Ann—William Eddington and John Fry together could send only enough passage money for Ann and three, possibly four, of the children.

"Impossible," Ann exclaimed. "We must all go together, or none of us can go. Will would never abide the situation. Once he had part of us here and the others in Zion, he'd see that the rest of us would never leave."

"I was sure you'd feel that way, and I believe you have cause," David murmured. "I'll respond at once, begging them to make further effort."

Once again Ann was left suspended. Nothing was definite, except that David Kimball had no doubt whatever that Ann was to leave this spring with the contingent of Saints.

Ann felt as though she was tethered to a hot air balloon—pulled first here, then there by the demands of those around her. She had never felt less in control. Her only anchor was her faith and the strength she received from her prayers.

It was late in April on a drizzly afternoon when David Kimball brought word that John Fry and William Eddington had sent all the money needed for the whole family. In bits and pieces Ann began packing small bundles of clothing and supplies and sending them to branch members to keep for her until the sailing date. The fear of Will's discovering their plans grew until it brought a constant metallic taste in her mouth.

Ann ached to talk about it all with someone, and wanted to tell the children, but there were too many of them to be trusted with such an explosive secret. She decided at least to tell Lydia, and begged her to guard the news carefully.

Lydia was thrilled at first, then sobered quickly.

"Must we leave father?" she asked.

Ann's eyes misted, her hard-won control very fragile. "Lydia, you know your father would not go with us, and would not allow us to leave if he were to find out. I despise having to deceive him, but he himself has made it necessary."

Lydia nodded sadly. She was torn between father and mother— and between love of the Church and love for her father. She knew her father loved her, loved each of his children in his own odd way, yet she knew how badly he had treated her mother. The love that had existed between them at first seemed to have been smothered by their differences. Nevertheless, Lydia cried at the thought of leaving her father behind.

David Kimball sent word that the ship was to sail in mid-May, anticipating the Saints' eventual arrival in the Salt Lake Valley by early

October. The first of May crept upon them, and Ann sent for Lydia to give notice to her employer and come home to help her get ready. Mary Ann, who made the better wage, was to keep working until the last moment. When Will questioned Lydia's presence at home once again, he was told it was a temporary arrangement while Lydia's employers were away.

Ann struggled with the burden of the dangerous secret and caring for William too. He was now so ill he could not lie down in bed and get his breath. Ann propped him up, yet every breath was a struggle. With their expected sailing date only a week away, Ann realized she would have to find someone to be with William while Will was at the dockyards. There was no one in the branch to whom she could turn—anyone in a position to help seemed to be leaving with them. *I've got to find someone,* Ann stewed. *He's helpless as a baby.* And with that thought came an idea. Mary Ann Bray! It had been years since Ann had used her midwifery, but surely she would look in on William if Ann left her a few coins. She sought her out at the first opportunity.

"'Tis to America ye be goin'? W'out your 'usband?" she frowned disapprovingly at Ann.

"Mary, I know how it must look. But you know there is little happiness for Will and me. I have two children in America, and a grandchild I've never seen. I know it's best that the children and I go, too."

"When do ye expect to be leavin'?"

"The ship sails on May 17—less than a week away."

"I'm not one to turn me back on the sick and dying." Her words cut into Ann sharply. "You'll be doin' what you're after doing, advice or no, but I'll see to your brother."

Ann thanked her warmly, pressed several coins into the woman's large hand, and then pleaded, "You understand it will go badly for me if Will discovers my plan."

"Aye, I'm not daft, missus, nor dumb. Your secret's safe with Mary Ann Bray."

Once again Ann nodded her thanks and quickly took her leave. That last problem seemingly taken care of, Ann had now only to wait at home for the day when she would hustle all the children and herself to the train station, and thence to London and Shadwell docks. The waiting nearly stifled her. She made William as comfortable as possible, sent Will off every morning to work and saw him home at night, cooked, caught up on mending she had held back from being packed, and worried. She slept fitfully at night, tossing and stirring about, only to dream frightening dreams she could not remember the next morning. She was terrified that Will would discover her plans, thrilled at the prospect of finally going, uncertain at leaving so much behind, inconsolably guilty at the thought of deserting both Will and William.

On the day before they were to leave, a branch member sent word that the ship's sailing had been delayed for two weeks. Ann breathed a measured sigh of relief, yet knew it only extended the anxiety and added to it.

She turned more and more attention to William, having done all she could to ready herself and the children. She spent hours now during the day at the kitchen table, a chair turned to watch William's every move. He called to her one day in a raspy whisper. "Ann, Ann."

"What is it, dear? May I get you something?"

"No, no—I—want—you—to—know—it's—all right," he labored to speak, then gasped for air.

"What's all right, William?" She stroked his head.

He struggled to speak again. "America," he managed to whisper, then closed his eyes.

Ann knelt at his bedside and held his hand, tears streaming down her cheeks. "Thank you, thank you," she murmured over and over. He knew, and he did not hold it against her. She, who had tried to ease his burden, was now comforted and relieved of the awful burden of guilt she felt at leaving her dying brother.

"America" proved to be the last word William uttered. Within a few hours he slipped into a coma, and Ann knew he was beyond feeling any more pain. Two days later he died, and was finally at rest.

Recognition of answered prayer again flooded Ann's being. In gratitude she knelt, knowing she would now not be required to leave William suffering, with only Will and a stranger to care for him.

Strange, she thought as she stood at the graveside, *we must learn some lessons over and over. How often I've been lifted in prayer, rescued through prayer, comforted, and guided—yet still I doubt and wonder, only to be taught again and again that the Lord knows our needs.* The funeral service left Ann calm and peaceful, spiritually tranquil, and aware of the Lord's intervention in her life as never before. With her face serene and thoughtful, she walked briskly into the sea-laden breeze, out of the cemetery, her chin high, her gaze steady.

13

May 31 to June 3, 1864

How I've longed to thy bosom to flee
Hymns, no. 145

The long night slowly gathered up its long black cloak, revealing the pale blue-gray underskirt of morning. It had been difficult for Lydia to sleep. She listened to the muffled sounds of her mother moving about the kitchen, preparing her father's usual morning meal of tea and porridge. Everything was just the same as always, yet everything was different. It was her last night in this bed, in this flat, in this city. She lay still and stiff-jointed, not wanting to disturb Emily, who had curled herself into a tight ball, rolled snugly against her sister, and pinned Lydia to the wall. Since Lydia's employment outside her home, both of them had become accustomed to sleeping alone, a luxury that had been frightening at first, but now would definitely have been more comfortable.

Not being able to sleep, Lydia wanted very much to get up, to walk into the kitchen, to watch her father eat his breakfast and leave for work. She wanted to put her arms around him and tell him how much she loved him, but it would all have been too unusual and would have alerted him to their plans. Was Zion worth a father, she wondered. What price had her mother already paid? What more would it cost in terms of home, husband, country? All Lydia knew was that her mother loved her and loved the Church. Where she led, Lydia would follow—and trust. She considered no other possibility.

In the kitchen Ann marveled that Will could be so unaware of the frantic pounding of her heart. If he could not see it beating under her bibbed apron, surely he could hear it! Its accelerated pounding blocked out every other sound in her own ears. She had to concentrate on acting normally.

Will ate slowly, methodically, as he did every morning. Ann wanted to urge him to hurry, yet she dreaded his finishing, for then he would go to the peg behind the kitchen door for his cap, nod briefly to Ann, and disappear out the door. She knew it had to happen. There was no turning back, yet she wanted to hold on to the moment a little while longer. Perhaps something of what she was feeling would communicate itself to Will. How do you silently bid goodbye to an unknowing husband? How can you transmit your feelings—the tumbled, jumbled, mishmash of emotion that churned within her—the anticipation, the guilt, the reluctance, the fear, the inevitability. There were no words to say, no way to say them if words could come, no time to say them if she could find the way. It was as though John and Sarah Jane and Fanny were leaving again—she boiled inside with a thousand thoughts, and could utter not a one. The note she had prepared would have to say it all.

Will stacked his dishes, rose slowly and with obvious effort from his chair, took down his cap, set it carefully upon his graying head, nodded to Ann, and walked out the door. The click of the latch was as startling to Ann as if a gun had been fired. She ran to the door, ready to call to Will—*be careful, don't overdo, take care of yourself*—but her hand never released the latch, and she stood instead, her burning forehead pressed against the wooden door.

Within moments she was shaking the children, rousing them, urging them to hurry.

"Emily, wake up—wake up. Do you want to go to Zion?"

"Zion? When?"

"Now!"

"To Zion? Now?"

"Yes, hurry and dress. We must away to the train station by eight sharp."

"But father—?"

"Father won't be going. Just hurry now." And Ann was gone to another bed to repeat the scene.

Mary Ann was the first to leave. Even the neighbors must not suspect their plans, for it was always possible one of them might feel it his duty to run to the shipyards to alert Will. Mary Ann often left early in the morning to return to work after a visit home. Ann kissed her daughter, noting with relief the sparkle in her eyes and her obvious anticipation.

David and Joe were next to go, as though on their way to school. Their faces, too, were alight with the adventure.

Lydia gathered up her sack of provisions. She hugged her mother at the door.

"Act naturally, dear. If someone should ask you where you are going or what you have in the sack, you must pretend to be delivering clothes."

For a long moment they looked at one another. Wordlessly each noted the other's pain and fought the impulse to cry. Ann patted Lydia's arm. "The twins and I will be along before you know it, and by then Mary and the boys will be at the station."

Lydia managed a shaky smile, stepped through the door her mother held open to her, and climbed the cold stairwell out of the damp basement flat. She paused for just a moment to look back. It had not been the happiest place—it was dark, dreary, and held little comfort, but it had been home, the only one she had ever known. Father would be returning here tonight, and he would find it empty. She ached for him, yet she could not wish he were going along. She could not remember a time she had not been aware of the low murmur of voices from her parents' bedroom, voices that usually became louder, filled with anger, explosive with hurled threats and bitter accusations. More often than not her father would curse his wife and her religion, then propel himself from the house in a rage. She loved her father, but she hated the strife. She sighed—in relief, in grief, in acceptance. She turned and walked rapidly toward the station.

There was no question about the twins' feelings. They danced and fidgeted until Ann thought seriously of tying them down until it was time to leave. She dared not send them with any of the others. In their great excitement, they would be sure to blurt out the whole story. Concern for keeping them in control kept a tight rein on Ann's emotions as she gathered up her last package, laid her note on the table, closed the door to the flat, and strode resolutely away.

The note had taken Ann hours of agonizing, writing and rewriting.

Dear Will:
Whether this message will in any manner help you understand what we have done I don't know. I only know I cannot leave without expressing some of what is in my heart.

We have had a strange love, my husband. I do not doubt

that you pursued your unbending course believing it to be out of love. I, too, have only sought to fulfill my love for you and our children through a course that somehow has never managed to intersect or merge with yours.

I hold no ill will toward you. On the contrary, I am grateful to you for helping me achieve a faith I may otherwise never have gained had you not forced me to look long and hard at the religion I know now means more than my life to me.

I cannot say I leave with no regrets, for that would be untrue. I regret with all my heart that we were unable to come to a unity in the faith. You must believe no other Power than that I follow now could impel me to break the vows we made at marriage.

Could my prayers alone have wrought your conversion, you would be with us at this moment. Those prayers will not cease at our separation. May God bless and keep you in His tender mercy.

Ann

Within minutes Ann and the children were reunited, the tickets were bought, and the bellowing engine rushed clacking into the station. Once they were all settled on the train, and the twins happily occupied peering out the windows, Ann breathed a huge sigh of relief. The first awful, wonderful, frightening step was accomplished. She was really on her way to Zion—all six of her children about her.

Yet nearly at once a nagging fear began to creep upon her. She had panicky moments when she had to turn to see who might be behind her. Had a neighbor seen them leave? Had Will been notified? Would he shortly be purchasing his own ticket at the station in pursuit of them?

Ann reasoned with herself. Even if he were aware of their departure, he most certainly could not have boarded the train. He would have to wait for a later one. And by the time a second train could reach London, Ann and the Saints would be safely aboard the ship. And by the time Will could possibly determine what dock, and what ship, it would have sailed. Ann forced herself to accept the logic of it.

She turned her eyes to look out the window. England sped by in all shades of green and vistas of quiet beauty. She tried to memorize every scene, fasten indelibly in her heart every setting, engrave in her mind's eye every landscape. She knew she would never see them again.

The four hours to London seemed to evaporate, and suddenly they were thrust into the thick of the sights and sounds of the world's largest city. She assigned each of the children a partner—Mary Ann to Elijah, Lydia to Emily, David to Joseph. They were to stay close together, never out of sight of one another. Ann, her short stature a handicap as people everywhere thronged the streets, tried repeatedly to hail a carriage, only to be shouldered aside time after time. But at last she was successful, and the seven of them climbed excitedly into the carriage, Emily and Elijah still agog from their maiden train ride and now thrilled to be aboard their first carriage.

"Shadwell docks," Ann instructed the driver. He nodded and touched his whip to his top hat, then flicked it briefly over the horse's back, and the carriage lurched into motion. The twins squealed in delight.

Ann, too, looked about her eagerly. London was not a city to be ignored. The carriage wove precariously in and out of the heavy traffic, and Ann gasped frequently at what she would have called "near disasters," but which the driver seemed to take in stride with hardly a nod of his head.

"Oh my yard, would ya' look at that!" Elijah exclaimed as he jumped up, nearly toppled over, and then was clamped back down in his seat by Mary Ann. All heads turned, but whatever it was he saw was swallowed up in the press of the crowded streets, and there were soon new sights to assail their eyes and capture their attention.

There were no fewer people about the docks. Men and women milled everywhere. Ann paid the driver and clambered uncertainly from the carriage, looking fearfully about her.

"Mum, look—it's Brother Kimball! He's waving to us," Lydia shouted.

Relieved to see a familiar face, they broke into a run, dodging in and out of walking and wandering people. They gathered breathlessly around his comforting figure.

"Which is our ship, Brother Kimball?" Ann asked as her eyes darted from one area to another.

"It's the *Hudson*, mother, but its departure has been delayed. It will be at least four more days before you can board."

A cry escaped Ann's lips, and her hand flew to her throat. Four days! Four days was a lifetime. Will could find them easily in four days, and he would not be above using the law to force them all back to Portsmouth.

"Come with me," David spoke loudly, above the hubbub of the harbor. "We'll find a place for you and the children to stay."

Blindly Ann followed where David Kimball led. Within an hour he had located a garret room, high above the first floor of a coffeehouse. They would be crowded, but it was shelter, and food was available downstairs. Ann sank onto the first cot she found in the room. She was unbelievably exhausted. Even the longest day bent over the hottest washtub had not wearied her as this day already had.

Lydia flew to the round window in the garret wall. "Look, Mum! You can see about the harbor. It's like a great forest!"

The children rushed to see. Their room looked out over the Thames and what appeared to be hundreds of ships at anchor. Their masts stuck nakedly into the air, like trees defoliated by a winter wind.

In spite of her weariness, Ann gathered the children about her, and they knelt in prayer. She had so much to be grateful for, yet the fear had returned. Zion was still a very long way off.

The children begged to go out.

"Mum, please! We'll never see London again. Please let us walk about! We won't go far," each of them pleaded in turn.

Ann was adamant. "No! We can't risk it. Your father could be out there looking for you. He'd snatch you away in a thrice. Absolutely not!"

Ann kept them all inside. They had all they presently needed within the walls of the coffeehouse. They could purchase their meals downstairs, sleep upstairs, and they could open the garret window for fresh air. There was little room, it was true, but the children at length made the most of it and resorted to quiet games and recitation of every silly rhyme they could recall:

Burn ash-wood green,
'Tis fire for a Queen;
Burn ash-wood sare,
'Twool make a man swear.

and

Snag, snag, put out your horn,
and I will give you a barleycorn.

Ann barely heard the constant repetition. She paced the floor or sat silently listening for footsteps on the stair. She rehearsed a dozen confrontation scenes with Will, and her imagination ran wild as she considered, then discarded, several different possibilities. She remembered with a sudden chill when he'd threatened her and their infant son with an ax, could hear again the many times they'd argued and his frightening ultimatums. *I'll see us all dead before I allow any of us to leave England.* The phrase echoed in her head. *See us all dead, see us all dead.* As each hour passed, her anxiety grew. The nights were long, and she slept little, dozing fitfully, only to start at the barest suggestion of a noise, a creaky stair, a shutter banging nearby. The din of the city abated somewhat at night, but what must certainly be scores of territorial battles between dogs, cats, and street urchins made up for the lack of usual daytime noises.

June 1 dragged inexorably by, and June 2 closed them all securely in a blanket of fog so dense it was as though a huge hand had pressed wads of thick wool against the window. The children had quieted down and dozed intermittently on their cots, the excitement worn thin, the waiting interminable for them, too.

Ann wondered how much longer it would be. Her heart fluttered within her at every sound, and she feared it would suddenly stop beating if the suspense were strung out much longer. And it did seem to stop when in the afternoon of June 2 a knock sounded at the door.

Ann jumped to her feet. "Hark," she ordered the children. There was no sound in the room, only the echo of the frantic knock upon the door. The color drained from Ann's face, and she clutched one hand with the other to still their trembling.

"Sister Littlefield," came the familiar voice through the door. It was David Kimball.

Ann rocked for a moment on her feet, then whispered, "Mary, let him in."

He bounded into the room totally unaware of their anxiety.

"Tomorrow! The ship sails tomorrow!"

"Heaven be praised," Ann breathed. "I was beginning to doubt I'd survive this wait."

"Look at this," he waved a paper at her. "Headlines announcing the departure of the *Hudson* as of May 31! Will most certainly will have read his paper! He'll think you've already sailed!"

Ann's relief was nearly tangible. She sat back down on the cot and fanned herself with the folded paper. David Kimball instructed them on the procedure for the following day, and Ann smiled and nodded, numb with the sudden release of anxiety, but grateful for his presence and help.

Lydia was the first to arise on June 3. She peered once again out the garret window. The fog of the previous day had lifted, but small tufts of it had snagged on the tops of the masts as the ships rocked gently in their allotted harbor space.

David Kimball gathered them all up and led them to the *Hudson*.

"I've registered you under your former married name, Fry," he explained to Ann. "It's just a precaution."

Ann nodded her approval. She looked anxiously about the dock as she climbed carefully along the gangplank. Traces of fear still clung to her. She'd lived with it so intimately for the past few weeks, she wondered if it would ever yield, no matter what the evidence of safety. After helping Ann register herself and the children with the boarding officer, David led them down to the third deck of the ship, where, as yet another precaution, they were hidden behind large accumulations of luggage. Knowing David felt the need for them to hide even at this point did little to dissipate Ann's trepidation.

With clammy hands she shook David's hand in farewell. He bent and kissed her forehead. "God speed, mother." In a husky whisper he murmured, "I'll miss the lot of you." Ann was surprised to see tears in his eyes.

The ship began to rock gently, and the twins' eyes opened wide as they realized they were on their way at last. Lydia gripped Mary Ann's arm and Joseph and David exchanged grins. As the tug pulled them slowly out of the harbor, they were taken before the ship's doctor, who examined them and their clothes carefully. Then they were allowed to see the commissarian, who issued them food rations for a week—hardtack, corned beef, rice, brown sugar, oatmeal, coffee, and tea.

At length all the Saints gathered on the top deck, in spite of an intermittent rain. They waved to the spectators who lined the wharf for quite a distance down the river. The passengers soon became quiet, gathering in small groups to talk. Some distance down the river, the tug paused in its efforts. They had arrived at Gravesend, from where the *Hudson* would strike out on its own.

A dozen or more tearful goodbyes were uttered as several elders, their missions not yet completed, left the *Hudson's* deck and their beloved converts to return to London with the tug. As it chugged gently away, the Saints waved, wiped tears from their eyes, and blew reddened noses. At length, in a spontaneous outburst, they all joined in three long, loud cheers that rang along the banks of the Thames and echoed from the distant hills.

In answer the missionaries returned their own vigorous three cheers—hip-hip-hooray, hip-hip-hooray, hip-hip-hooray—and waved their handkerchiefs. At once, everyone on board dug about in pockets, reticules, and sleeves, and produced a handkerchief. The deck of the *Hudson* came alive with hundreds of fluttering swaths of white cloth waving at the receding tug in an exultant token of love.

14

June 1864 to August 1864

*Think not when you gather to Zion,
your troubles and trials are through*
Hymns, no. 21

"All in favor, please signify by a voice vote," Elder John M. Kay shouted to the hordes of Saints crowded on the upper deck. A chorus of ayes answered back and, there being none who disapproved, the *Hudson's* company of Saints became duly organized with Elder Kay as president and George Halliday, John L. Smith, and Matthew McCune as counselors. After a considerable number of announcements, directions, and admonitions, a majority of the Saints returned to their assigned decks.

Ann lingered, looking once again for the twins. She wished that Captain Pratt had been more strict, but the jovial man did not seem to mind that his ship had become, at certain times, a playground for dozens of scampering youngsters. The weather so far had been good, and the children's boundless curiosity led them from one end of the ship to the other, from one deck to another. In spite of Ann's, Mary Ann's, and Lydia's watchful care, Elijah and Emily disappeared at every opportunity.

While she knew they could not become lost, Ann feared they would fall overboard. Her heart thumped wildly every time she saw one of them leaning over the rail, watching the wake as it roiled away from the ship.

"Mum, there's to be a choir on board, and songs both morning and evening. May I sing with them?" Lydia questioned her mother.

"La, what a fine idea! Just see to it that if Mary Ann wants to join too that one or the other of you keeps after the twins. I'm at wit's end trying to keep track of those two, even with the help of the both of you."

"Oh, Mum, what a lark!" Lydia exclaimed, and ran off to report to the choir director, a young man from London by the name of George Careless.

Ann spotted the twins high up on the poop deck, watching intently as a seaman demonstrated his knot-tying prowess. They seemed occupied for the moment, and Ann's worry eased up. The first two or three days at sea had been going amazingly well. Neither Ann nor the children had been seasick. That seemed to be a rare blessing, for no sooner had the ship passed Margate and into the open sea than passengers all around them began dashing to the rail. Ann suspected that their luck was due partly to the fact they had not stoked up on food the way most of the passengers had—Ann had had to pinch every pence of their meager funds. Their stomachs had been only lightly filled.

Aside from a few brief personal chores each morning, the gathering to prayers both morning and evening, and the necessity of rationing out the food supply at mealtimes, Ann's life aboard ship was relatively unburdened. The freedom was a mixed blessing. It seemed at once both delightful and slightly sinful. Yet it left room, too, for the worry to creep back into the recesses of her heart. The chances were good that Will had read the notice of the ship's sailing four days earlier than it actually had, but Ann had no way of knowing that with absolute surety. Even so, what would he do then? The ship was still within sight of land. They were heading northward, sailing along the coast. The *Hudson* was a large ship, not nearly as fast as many clippers and mail packets that crisscrossed the Atlantic. There was still the chance that Will could be purchasing passage on one of them, ready to follow them. The tossing ship only echoed Ann's uneasy feelings.

Yet there were diversions. Of the more than eight hundred Saints aboard, many were from the Southampton Conference. Ann recognized and renewed acquaintances with many of them, and with those from neighboring branches as well. She had been particularly delighted to recognize Elizabeth Downham of Basington Branch. Her son Charles was of the same age as Elijah and Emily, and the trio had been nearly inseparable immediately. The two women exchanged sympathetic chatter on the difficulty of keeping track of their offspring.

The ship seemed to lay lightly in the water, despite its size and the weight of both cargo and passengers. There had been no lack of wind to keep them moving, yet they still clung to England's coastline. Ann felt she would rest easier when she could no longer see land. Now that the adventure was started, there was nothing to do but finish it. She wanted as much distance between the seven of them and England as possible.

As Ann rinsed their utensils in the water barrel on the third deck after their morning meal, she heard David's voice squeaking at her. At fifteen, David was enduring the discomfort and embarrassment of a voice change. He never knew what was going to come out when he opened his mouth to speak.

"Mum, you should come up on deck. You'll want to see this," he called excitedly to her.

"Can't it wait, David? It takes time to wait my turn for the water barrel."

"Right away, Mum. There's a little boat coming after us."

Ann dropped the cup she'd been rinsing. Her face paled, and she nodded quickly to David that she would come at once. She gathered up her utensils, hurried back to their berths, and tossed the entire collection quickly atop the blanket of the bottom berth. She touched a trembling hand to each temple and smoothed the hair back from her face.

"It can't be Will, it can't be," she muttered to herself. Yet her heart beat wildly, and she could scarcely think. She pulled herself shakily up the steps to the second, then the main, deck.

Ann watched every movement of the small craft, each lift of its oars, as it drew gradually closer and closer to the *Hudson*. At length the boat drew near enough for Ann to see that it held two men—one man at the oars, his back to them, and another facing the oarsman. Ann watched until her eyes stung from the concentrated staring. She blinked rapidly several times, then seemed to melt into a fluid mass as she reached for David's arm.

"It's not your father," Ann managed to croak. They stepped back from the rail as a crew member lowered a rope ladder for a lone passenger to board.

"It's not Father," David echoed.

"Thank God!" Ann quavered, and sent that heartfelt prayer fervently heavenward.

After that frightful moment, Ann's stomach churned for quite a while. But soon, she noted gratefully, the ship had changed course.

They were sailing now due west, and soon not even Ireland could be seen any longer.

Within a few days of their altered course came a change in their shipboard lives also.

"Measles!" Joseph exclaimed. "I thought you couldn't board this thing if you was sick."

"That's why we were all 'zamined, 'tweren't it, Mum," Emily pronounced solemnly.

"Well, someone slipped on board carrying 'em, 'cause a lot of people are getting very sick," Lydia affirmed.

By the third week in June, scores of cases of measles were reported over the entire ship. Ann forgot her own private worries and turned to nursing the sick and helping mothers with sick children. She kept her own out of the way, and the Captain ordered all the sick removed to a single area on one deck in a effort to isolate the disease.

Both young and old seemed to be affected, but the children seemed to suffer the most and were particularly vulnerable to the high fever. Fortunately a good supply of water was aboard, and the Captain issued no restrictions on use of it. The *Hudson* was well equipped with an excellent condensing machine and provided fresher, better-tasting water than could be had in many parts of England. Ann helped bathe the affected children's heads, cooling down their rash-reddened bodies with dampened cloths. But in spite of the combined efforts of several of the sisters, the disease, or complications associated with it, began to claim its victims.

By early in July four children and one woman had died. The children were all less than two years of age, and included a three-month-old baby girl. The Saints gathered on deck for the funeral services.

Ann wept openly at the sight of the tightly wrapped and weighted bodies, lined up precisely on the deck, one large one, four tiny ones. Elder Kay gave the funeral sermon.

"The ties that unite us," he spoke out firmly, "are stronger than death, and the love that warms honest, upright hearts lives and grows beyond the grave. The strength of parental affection is increased, and when earth's fleeting joys and transient scenes shall have passed away, the links now broken in the family chain by death's chilly hand shall be again welded together. It matters not materially where the body lays, whether beneath the greensward in its fatherland, or away, far from the haunt of men, in the deep, dark bed of the ocean."

Lydia, too, sobbed to see the white bundles slipped rapidly off a plank into the depths of the sea.

At the choir's presentation the next morning Brother George Careless introduced a new hymn.

"Brother Parley P. Pratt wrote the words, with which we are all familiar, but I have written new music for this hymn," Brother Careless announced. In a clear, melodic voice, he sang the new music, the choir joining in as they became familiar with it. Lydia found the words comforting, and the promise hopeful.

The morning breaks, the shadows flee;
Lo, Zion's standard is unfurled!
The dawning of a brighter day
Majestic rises on the world.

The last verse, particularly, echoed in Lydia's heart, and she sought her mother's eyes as she sang:

Angels from heaven and truth from earth
Have met, and both have record borne;
Thus Zion's light is bursting forth
To bring her ransomed children home.

Home! Lydia thought. Home! Zion was home. They were all on their way home.

"I double-dare yer," Charles Downham taunted Elijah.

"I triple-dare yer back," Elijah answered, as Emily looked on in wonder.

"You had no-ought. Mum will huff you good," Emily warned.

The three of them stood beside a hoisted lifeboat.

"I will if'n you will," Charles offered.

"Done," Elijah retorted, and simultaneously the two of them began clambering into the lifeboat. Emily hung back, unsure of just where these two might lead her.

"Come on. Bythen they find us, we'll have grigged about a bit."

Responding to their encouragement, Emily put up her hands to be helped into the boat. Charles stood and leaned over to grab her. Suddenly the boat pitched wildly. Elijah hung on for dear life, but Charles was pitched headlong out of the boat and flung down to the main deck. Emily screamed as Elijah climbed gingerly out of the swaying boat and back to the safety of the poop deck. The two of them scrambled down between the gathering passengers to stand over Charles.

Amid cries to send for Mr. Rogers, the ship's doctor, Elijah shuddered with fear. "Is he dead?" he managed to croak.

A moan escaped Charles's lips. "No, son, 'e's not dead. But from the looks o' that arm, I'd say it's broken of a surety."

Ann wanted to shake the two of them. When she'd heard the outcry that a young boy had fallen from the deck, she rushed up from below to see the twins standing ashen-faced over Charles. But one look at them, and Ann knew they were already suffering enough. Ann had little trouble keeping them close to her for a few days after the accident.

The days seemed to move along quickly. Ann still helped now and then with the remaining measles cases. The Captain sent down quantities of soup, made from preserved meat, for the benefit of the sick. It proved to be quite nourishing and tasty, though four more children died despite their best efforts.

The *Hudson* was passed by several other ships en route, and at each sighting Ann worried anew whether Will might not be on board. All the money he had saved could now be used to purchase passage on the fastest available ship. Ann told herself it was ridiculous to suppose such a thing, but the persistence of the notion was difficult to shake. "Will is a moderate, temperate man and does naun on impulse," she argued with herself. Then would come the vision of him standing in the doorway with the ax raised, ready to cut them down. At the heart of the matter, Ann knew Will was capable of almost anything when pushed to the limit.

Yet except for one steamer, recognized by the crew as a Confederate privateer, which turned two or three times near them as if trying to decide to board them or not, none of the ships seemed to pay them much mind and continued on their way. Aside from a quickly contained galley fire one day, there were no other shipboard incidents, and the *Hudson* ploughed steadily westward. Late in the afternoon of July 18, the long anticipated cry went up.

"Land, land! Land, ho!"

Mary and Lydia rushed topside. There in the distance was a slim outline on the western horizon. "America!" Lydia repeated under her breath, over and over.

As night fell on the *Hudson*, Brother Kay gathered the Saints together for prayer and singing.

"Fellow Saints, the first long and arduous part of our journey is near an end. Tomorrow we shall be towed into Castle Gardens in New York. We shall give you further instruction at our prayer service in the morning; tonight let us offer up our grateful thanks to the Lord for the protection and care extended us thus far, that with confidence we may move on, realizing he will still befriend us, and his bright smile of compassionate love and fondness continue to gladden our hearts as we tread the extended prairies, or climb the mountain steeps, on our way to the hallowed home of the Saints.

"A word of warning to each—America is, as you are aware, in the midst of a civil war. Keep your wits about you and do not stray from one another nor your appointed leaders."

Joseph and David exchanged glances, as did the girls. They could not conceive of any possible problems now that they had crossed a great ocean, survived the measles, the twins' adventures, and a fire in the galley. Yet they soon found that Brother Kay's warnings were not idle words.

As the *Hudson* drew closer to the harbor, what appeared to be swarms of small boats began moving toward them. Alarmed, Ann questioned Brother Singleton, who explained that most of the boats were anxious to sell fresh food and trinkets to the passengers. Ann cautioned the children to stay away from the portholes as every little boat seemed to be sending up its own grappling hook and jockeying for a favored position in order to traffic with the passengers.

Lydia thought they reminded her of pirates. "If they only want to sell us goods, Mum, what are the knives and pistols for?"

Alarmed, Ann ran to the porthole. Brother Singleton followed after.

One large boat had managed to send its men on board armed with knives and pistols, as Lydia had seen. There was a sudden rush into the lower decks by those who had been lining the rails on the upper deck. Lydia, David, and Joseph gathered around the breathless escapees.

"What did they want?"

"Who are they?"

"Where did they come from?"

"Are they pirates?"

Everyone seemed to be talking at once. Brother Singleton calmed everyone down and confirmed his own thoughts. "These men want to capture as many men as they can and sell them into service in the army. It's called conscription."

"You mean if they had grabbed President Kay or you or any of the men, they would have sold him and made him fight for somebody else?" Joe asked.

"That's right, young nipper," Brother Singleton affirmed. "But the captain seems to have everything under control now. The boarders have been sent packing, and seem to have gone away empty-handed," he said as he surveyed the scene from the porthole.

Exciting though the event had been, it made many of the Saints uneasy. For two days the company stayed aboard the ship. Then it slowly began moving again. They were at last being towed into Castle Gardens.

Many of the passengers began throwing their old provisions over the rail. Ann was appalled, and rushed to request that some of them be given to her instead of dumped. She was very worried about their money. The unexpected four-day delay in London had reduced their meager funds. Anything she could save on food from here on out would be that much better for their situation.

Castle Gardens was an island, used primarily to screen new arrivals to the United States to be sure they were free from disease and that they had proper immigration papers. Ann and the children were delighted to be once again on firm ground, but the wait lengthened interminably. The processing of their papers seemed to take forever, and the fact that more than eight hundred others were in the same position was little consolation. But at last, all paperwork duly processed and authorized, the Saints were taken to flatboats that ferried them up the Hudson River to Albany. The children lost no opportunity to soak up their first days of sight-seeing in America.

In Albany, Ann was directed to the train on which they were to travel to St. Joseph, Missouri. She was astonished to discover they would be on the train for two weeks.

"Two weeks! My yard, how big is this country? We can travel the length of England in a day or two!"

The children stationed themselves at windows and ogled the scenery. America began to mean endless land to them. Their perception of England grew smaller and smaller, and less and less distinct. The food Ann had rescued from being disposed of on the *Hudson* lasted for nearly all their train journey. It finally gave out two days before they reached St. Joseph.

"We must be careful, children," Ann cautioned. "We must conserve every pence, every farthing, if we are to complete our journey."

"Not pence, Mum," Elijah taunted. "It's penny here in America."

"Don't be impersome, Elijah," his mother warned. Then she smiled. "But you are right, we must learn new ways now."

Elijah grinned back at her, and all the children nodded their agreement.

"We're used to making do, Mum," Mary Ann assured her.

"It'll all come round," David spoke with the authority of the oldest male in the family. His phrase was a startling reminder of Will. How often Ann had heard him use those same words!

And how the thought of her husband once again sent tremors of worry along her veins. Would she ever be free of the anxiety?

At last the big black engine puffed into St. Joseph, Missouri, and the porter called out, "End of the line, folks. We don't go no fu'ther."

The next leg of their journey was once again by flatboat. Ann was totally confused. Her surroundings were so unfamiliar, her sense of time and distance so bewildered, she would have hated to rely on her own judgment as to direction. She knew they had had to travel west on the ocean, and they had gone north along the Hudson River and generally west on the train to St. Joseph. Yet now the flatboats were pointed north. Ann sighed her frustration and hoped everyone knew what they were about. She certainly had no idea.

Once again Ann herded the children aboard the boat. She saw them all settled as comfortably as possible on packing crates, and warned the twins once again about staying close. They had no sooner settled down when an alarm sounded.

"The Rebels are upon us! Load up and push out!"

Instinctively Ann reached for her nearest child, then counted noses quickly. They had few enough belongings to worry about, but those too were safely on board. She watched as last-minute boarders scrambled to reach the safety of the flatboats. Just as the crew began poling them away from the shore the crackle of gunfire broke out. The Saints watched from the boats as they gradually pulled farther and farther from shore. Flames began licking about the buildings. Within moments most of St. Joseph seemed to be ablaze.

"Not a moment to spare," one of the brethren commented.

"We'd have been in a rare scamble if the rebs had come a mite sooner," another called out.

Ann finally dared breathe. She shivered involuntarily to think what could have happened had the flatboats been burned along with the city.

Fortunately, the trip upriver to Wyoming, Nebraska, continued without further incident.

"I've not heard of this Wyoming place we're on our way to," Ann questioned Brother Singleton, once again a shipmate.

"I understand it's replaced Florence as the outfitting station for the Saints. This is the first year it's been used."

116

"Yes, Florence—that's the place I've heard mentioned before," Ann recalled.

"Evidently Indian attacks along the Oregon Trail have encouraged Church leaders to establish this more southern staging area," he explained.

"Indians!" Ann exclaimed. "Can we expect problems with Indians, too?"

Brother Singleton smiled and put an arm around his wife, Amelia.

"It does seem a bit much, doesn't it? Measles aboard ship, rebels attacking and burning, and now Indian raids."

Ann closed her eyes and shook her head. "Faith," she murmured. She caught David's eye and cut off his remark before he could say it. "I know, I know. It will all come round."

Wyoming, Nebraska, proved to be a busy place. Every building seemed stuffed to overflowing with either goods to be freighted to the Valley, or with cargo to be sent along with or used by those traveling on to the goldfields in California. But in Wyoming, a small village on the west bank of the Missouri River, were the wagons and teams waiting to take them the last leg of the journey.

But it was also there that Ann came to the end of her funds. As the Church agent, Joseph W. Young contacted each family head and assigned each family to wagons, collecting money for foodstuffs, cooking supplies, and so forth. Experience had dictated that the families in each wagon have certain basic supplies. A complete wagon, team, tent and provisions could be outfitted for a minimum of $400 and went as high as $800. The provisions alone, of course, cost considerably less, but any amount was more than Ann had. Ann avoided meeting him as long as possible. She began to panic.

She called the children to her, and they gathered together for consultation.

"We can't have come this far, Mum, and have to give up," Lydia declared.

"We must have a prayer and decide what's best. Maybe we'll have to work awhile as John did in New York to gain sufficient funds to continue," Ann stated with more confidence than she felt. What jobs they would find or where they would stay were questions that boggled her mind and only added to her concern.

Nevertheless they all bowed their heads, and David voiced their joint concerns, praying for guidance, clear heads, and the wherewithal to continue their journey.

Comforted, Ann shepherded the children back toward Elder Young's office near the Church's two large warehouses. En route they passed the postal office. On impulse Ann turned in, and the children followed.

"May I help you?" the attendant asked.

"I'm not sure," Ann replied. "Would letters from Salt Lake Valley arrive here?"

"Yes, ma'am. You expectin' mail from the West?"

"Not exactly, but would you look to see if you have anything for me, Ann Littlefield."

The attendant picked up a stack of letters and began shuffling through them. Ann drummed the counter nervously with her fingers.

"You acquainted with a John Fry, ma'am?"

Ann's heart leaped to her throat. "Yes, yes, that would be it."

"Sign here, and the letter's yours."

Ann scratched her name hurriedly on the paper with a quill pen. She thanked the agent and turned quickly away. "Come, children. Let's see what John has to say."

Outside, the children gathered around their mother. With trembling fingers she ripped open the envelope and unfolded the letter. Another piece of paper fluttered to the ground. Joseph picked it up.

"Mum, look. Look what was in the letter!" They all turned their eyes from Ann to Joseph. "A fifty-dollar bill!"

15

August, September, and October 1864

God will strengthen thy feet

Hymns, no. 145

"Up you go, nipper," Hubert Singleton declared as he swung Elijah up onto the wagon seat. Then he reached for Emily and plopped her down behind the seat. Hubert was rounding up the smaller children in their party. The wagon was perched atop the beginning of a long, grassy decline. It was not a steep hill, but it seemed to descend for quite a distance, and Hubert's father, Brother Singleton, had decided the children could ride along without taxing the oxen.

Ann was grateful she was once again traveling with the Singletons. Not only were they familiar faces from Southampton Conference, but they had been cheerful shipmates and were constantly reassuring in answering Ann's many questions. Both Amelia and Ann had nursed the many sick children aboard the *Hudson*, including Amelia's granddaughter, her oldest son's child. The baby had died, and Ann had grieved along with the young couple, and with the baby's grandparents as well.

The Singletons had a large family: besides their eldest son, Frederick, and his wife, there were Albert, 21; Malinda, 19; Hubert, 16; Rosena, 14; Hercules, 11; Amelia, 9; and Leopold, not quite 3. Though it taxed the wagon's capacity to the fullest, the Singletons had been of one mind in welcoming the assignment of the Littlefields to their wagon. Altogether, they made a company of eighteen. Amelia and Leopold, the two youngest, were the children Hubert was now rounding up for their ride down the long hill.

Supplies plus the personal belongings of that many people meant that very few could ride in the wagon. Only the youngest children were occasionally accorded the privilege. Finally Hubert lifted Leopold up beside Emily, and Amelia scrambled up herself. Giggling and poking at one another, they jumped and jiggled, teased and taunted as they waited for Albert to climb aboard and drive them down the hill.

"Elijah," Ann called. "Don't twit the girls, and watch out for young Leopold there. He's just a baby."

But the warning came too late. In their rowdy horseplay Elijah kicked loose the brake, and the wagon began rumbling down the hill, forcing the oxen ahead of it. Albert, when alerted to the moving wagon, ran to climb aboard, but by the time he gathered his wits about him and gave chase, the wagon had picked up so much speed that the oxen were racing to keep from being overtaken.

Down the hill the wagon plummeted, the children bouncing back and forth between one another and against the sacks of provisions. Bundles began jouncing out the back of the wagon. Emily clung with one hand to a bow holding up the heavy white canvas over their heads and held onto Leopold's shirt with the other. Amelia squealed half in fear, half in delight, and Elijah grabbed hold of the forwardmost bow with both hands. He gaped with wide, dark eyes as the oxen galloped pell-mell down the hill, hollering all the way, "Oh, my yard! Oh, my yard!"

Finally the hill evened out, and the trembling oxen slowed, then stopped, heaving and panting. When the others caught up with the wagon, there was a moment of silence while quick surveys were taken to see who, if anyone, was hurt. When it was discovered all were unharmed, Amelia let out a little giggle, and pretty soon they were all laughing and hooting, the merriment a welcome relief from their fearful anxiety moments before.

When Lydia could speak once again, she remarked, "If that wagon hadn't stopped at the bottom of the hill, we'd soon have been in Zion—or someplace!"

Ann sat beside the road, holding her sides. She had not run, nor laughed, so hard in years. The trip this far had been far from easy, and it was good for them all to feel the delightful intoxication of unrestrained laughter. Every day seemed to bring a fair share of problems and worries. Yet every day marked off another twenty to twenty-five miles closer to Zion. Again Ann wondered at the immensity of America. It had already been weeks—weeks, not days!—they had traversed the continent, and still they were hundreds of miles from Zion.

Ann felt some concern for the Singleton family. They were tailors by trade, and the hard physical labor and the unaccustomed endless walking were affecting Brother Singleton. Even though Ann was forty-seven years of age, she seemed to be faring better than he, hardened for the journey by the long years of back-breaking labor she had endured in Portsmouth.

"I suppose I must be grateful to Will, in a way," Ann mused to herself as she trudged beside the wagon. "If not for his insistence that I work for the food in the family, I wonder if I'd be hardy enough for this trip."

As always, thoughts of Will brought the familiar pangs of guilt and anxiety. She no longer glanced over her shoulder for fear he would be behind her, but she could not help but wonder what he was doing. Had he set out after them? Would he, too, be trodding these same dusty wagon ruts trying to track her down? Was his hernia still causing him pain? Ann turned the questions over and over in her mind, but reached the same conclusion she had before. It did no good to speculate. She'd probably never know. Will and their life together in England was a closed chapter in her life. Once again she turned her attention to survival.

Each morning Ann was the first of their wagon to arise. She'd gather firewood if it was available, or buffalo chips if it was not, and start the cook fires. After a hasty and early breakfast, the long day's walk would begin.

The twins, when not riding, would make a dozen side trips during the day, and Ann was amazed at their resiliency. Amelia, too, commented that the children probably would wind up walking twice as far as the adults, for they were forever scrambling off to see from the top of this or that hill, to investigate a rabbit hole, or to chase a prairie dog. In all their wanderings, though, Ann cautioned them to stay in sight, and they were content to do so. Ann had not forgotten Brother Singleton's comments about Indian raids along the trail.

She was more apprehensive than surprised, therefore, when one morning the word ran through the company that Indians had been sighted. Already along the trail the company had seen a house or two burned to the ground, and crops scorched as well, and it was noised about that Indians had been responsible. Ann listened carefully to the instructions at the campfire that night. They were to ready the goods each wagon carried for possible trade with or gifts for the Indians. The tension thickened that next day as several Indians astride their horses appeared on a small rise to the north of the trail. They rode slowly toward the wagon train, and as they drew nearer, Ann could see that they were brightly attired in beaded clothing and feathered headdress.

"Soor, they really do get painted up," Joseph exclaimed to Elijah, whose eyes once again were wide with wonder.

They all watched warily, but just as suddenly as they had appeared, they veered off in a gallop and were soon only a puff of dust in the distance.

The wagon train nearly in unison exhaled in relief and once again moved on.

Gradually the Saints began to wear down. As September passed, illness began cropping up among them. Elder Kay, their company president on the *Hudson,* and still the Saints' presiding authority, was one of the first to be stricken. He seemed to fight the illness at first, and Sister Kay nursed him patiently in their wagon. Others seemed not to have the strength to fight, and every so often the train paused to dig a grave and leave behind one of their number. Near the Little Laramie, John Kay died, and on its bank they tearfully buried him.

The Saints plodded on. The plains of Nebraska fell behind them, and they trudged on into Wyoming country. The nights began getting cooler, and even the days held a certain chill that was becoming more and more difficult to walk off. As they gradually climbed toward the Rocky Mountains, Ann became increasingly impatient. *Endless,* she murmured to herself, *this country is endless. There is no Zion, only a perpetually dusty road that leads nowhere.* She began to dread the choking dust, yet the muddy trails left after a heavy soaking rain were worse.

Step by step, mile by mile, day after day, the last wagon train of the season pushed on. No one could stop, there was no talk of stopping, yet each weary traveler longed to do so. Even a few days' respite from the endless walking and mindless struggle to place one foot after another seemed a heavenly dream. At least it seemed so to Ann. Miles and miles of trail gradually slipped behind them.

Near Fort Bridger one of their own wagon fell ill with the sickness that had been plaguing so many in the company. Leopold, the youngest member of the Singleton family, seemed to be healthy one day and seriously stricken the next. Amelia nursed him carefully, and

Ann spelled her when needed. Despite their loving care, Leopold died three days after taking sick. Once again the company stopped to dig a small grave by the wayside.

Ann wept openly. So many lives lost along the way! By the grace of God, none of her own had been lost—thus far. Her prayers were filled with gratitude for the robust health of her children and herself, and with pleas for comfort for the Singletons, who were weary beyond belief, and who had already lost a granddaughter and a son to the unyielding, unrelenting, and unending road to Zion.

Amelia's husband, Francis, seemed to visibly wilt under the loss of his youngest son. Within days he, too, became ill. On October 22 he was buried by the side of the trail.

The evening campfires had become noticeably more restrained. There were fewer late-night chats, and even less horseplay and care-free frolic. The Saints' unrestrained enthusiasm, so evident at the beginning of their trek, had been tempered now by a stolid, serious determination to endure.

The campfires kept them all enlisted in their joint venture. When one of their number faltered, it was evident at the evening or morning gathering, and friends and neighbors bolstered, encouraged, and strengthened. Though there was little frivolous merriment among the adult Saints, there was nevertheless a fine-tempered, keenly honed, steel-edged determination to succeed, dust, death, or devilish temptations notwithstanding.

The Saints obtained with the miles a sure knowledge of the depth of their commitment, a knowledge that Ann had already obtained long before she left England. Around boulders, over ruts, across rivers, through mud, against wind, and now, ankle-deep into snow, Ann and her fellow Saints moved on, the wagons creaking and straining, groaning under their burdens.

It was late in October. The Singleton wagon and many others were camped along the Bear River. The evening meal had been eaten, and Mary Ann, Lydia, Malinda, and Rosena had fetched water from the river, heated it over the fire, and chattered while working together cleaning up the utensils and tin plates. The older Singleton boys and David and Joseph had gone off to gather with a few others to swap stories and compare notes on whatever subject happened to come up. The younger children scampered between neighboring wagons. Ann, as usual since Brother Singleton's death, stayed close to Amelia.

Neither of them had a husband now, and they found consolation in their conversations with one another. Amelia was particularly adept at drawing Ann out, though Ann often wondered who was comforting whom. When Ann remarked regarding Amelia's strength to continue in the face of the loss of her husband, son, and grandchild, Amelia answered, "It's what Francis wanted. If I gave up now, their deaths would be meaningless."

"Besides," she continued, "I need not look far before I see those who've lost more than I. I'd not trade places with anyone. I'm content with my lot."

"You've paid dear for Zion, Amelia," Ann commented.

"There's scarce a family on this train who hasn't paid dear," Amelia agreed. "What costs us most is what we hold most precious."

Ann nodded and wrapped her shawl more closely about her. The wind was coming up, and it whipped at the campfire, breaking up the flames, fanning them up into long streaks, then extinguishing them quickly.

"I've no regrets over the long of it," Ann mused. "Does it seem strange to you that I'd leave husband as well as home for Zion?"

Amelia looked at Ann. She studied her face, worn but alive with a vibrant strength and inner courage; her hands, permanently reddened from the years of hot water and harsh soap; her hair, streaked with gray. "If Nephi could be persuaded to lop off Laban's head that his family might live, who am I to question your leaving behind a man who would keep your family from living the gospel?"

Ann smiled. "'Better that one man should die than a nation perish in unbelief.' I suppose there are similarities," she said.

"You've done what had to be done. As we all have," Amelia answered.

"And it's soon accomplished," Ann sighed. "Brother Snow says we're less than a week from the Valley. It's only a matter of days now."

"Days! And then it will be hours. All things, good and bad, end sooner or later. Francis was fond of saying that nowhere in the Book of Mormon does it say, 'And it came to *stay*.' It always says 'And it came to *pass*.'"

Ann chuckled. "And this night is passing on, too. I'd best get the twins bedded down." She stood and stretched her back.

"Mum," she heard Emily call. The twins came running up to the wagon.

"Mum, there's a man asking for you," they both chattered in near unison. They turned to point out a tall figure striding into the pale circle of light surrounding the campfire.

Ann turned, stopped, frowned. As he drew nearer, her hands

flew to her face as she shouted in joy, "Johnny! Johnny, my boy, my son!" In an instant she was in his arms as he lifted her up and rocked her in a fierce embrace.

The twins hung back shyly, puzzled at their mother's warm reception of this stranger. At length Ann stood back and looked at Johnny from arm's length.

"I can't believe it! Johnny, is it really you?" She wiped at the tears that persisted in tumbling down her cheeks.

He grinned that lopsided grin so reminiscent of his father's and nodded. "Now tell me which Littlefields are over there staring holes in me, so we can all get reacquainted."

Shyly at first, then with increasing joviality Ann and Johnny and his long-separated brothers and sisters warmed to each other. More fuel was added to the campfire as they sat close, talked and laughed, cried and remembered. Ann devoured her son with her eyes, and occasionally reached out to touch his hand or arm. Her heart was full, her cup overflowing. Such joy had been rare in her life.

In the morning Ann hugged Amelia and bid goodbye to the Singletons. John had brought a buggy to whisk them all away to the Valley. They gathered a few belongings, left some in the wagon for the Singletons to bring in with them, and clambered happily into the buggy. John clucked to the horses, and they trotted briskly away from Bear River, smoothly and quickly eating up the remaining miles to Zion. After the endless walking, it seemed to Ann she had been plucked out of quicksand and perched delicately on silver wings, slipping and gliding effortlessly toward the promised land.

They stopped for the night at Coalville and ate what seemed to all to be a banquet with real vegetables, fruit, and molasses cake. Then back into the buggy they scrambled once again to rapidly consume the last few miles.

At the crest of the canyon trail, when the Valley lay spread out before them, John stopped the buggy. No words were necessary as Ann scanned the scene before her. Whitewashed adobe houses in neat rows, more substantial wood dwellings, orchards, and the sweet aroma of wood fires wafted up to fill their eyes and noses with poignant sights and scents.

Johnny reached over and took Ann's hand. With the other he shook the reins lightly, and the buggy thrust gently forward. "Welcome to Zion, Mother. Welcome home!"

Epilogue

February 18, 1865

To Mrs. Ann Littlefield
c/o the Mormons
Salt Lake City
America

You'll be after knowing about the mister. He asked my help to find a surgeon to fix his hernia. The doctor charged a fair middling of a fee, I'll tell you that, but the mister had no trouble in its payment. But for all his trouble, he passed on today after going under the knife. I did what I could for him.

I can't say as how I understand how you could desert husband and home to go to such a place as America, but then I'm not one to make judgments.

God speed you all wherever you are, and when you think of Mary Ann Bray, I hope it's with fondness.

I remain your always obedient servant,

Mary Ann Bray